Research On Teaching
Special Collection
138 Erickson Hall/MSU

W9-BEZ-461

From the Library of
Philip P. Kelly

Teacher Education Evaluation

Evaluation in Education and Human Services

Editors:

George F. Madaus, Boston College, Chestnut
Hill, Massachusetts, U.S.A.
Daniel L. Stufflebeam, Western Michigan
University, Kalamazoo, Michigan, U.S.A.

Previously published books in the series:

Teacher Education Evaluation

edited by

William J. Gephart
Jerry B. Ayers
Center for Teacher Education Evaluation
Tennessee Technological University

Kluwer Academic Publishers
Boston   Dordrecht   Lancaster

Distributors for North America:
Kluwer Academic Publishers
101 Philip Drive
Assinippi Park
Norwell, Massachusetts 02061, USA

Distributors for the UK and Ireland:
Kluwer Academic Publishers
Falcon House, Queen Square
Lancaster LA1 1RN, UK

Distributors for all other countries:
Kluwer Academic Publishers Group
Distribution Centre
Post Office Box 322
3300 AH Dordrecht, The Netherlands

Library of Congress Cataloging in Publication Data

Teacher education evaluation.

(Evaluation in education and human services)
Papers from a conference entitled Teacher
Education Program Evaluation: some Missing Links,
held May 17-19, 1987, in Nashville, Tenn.
Includes index.
1. Teachers—Training of—United States—Evaluation—
Congresses. I. Gephart, William J. II. Ayers, Jerry B.
III. Series.
LB1715.T413 1988   370'.7'1   88-2992
ISBN 0-89838-270-X

Copyright © 1988 by Kluwer Academic Publishers. Second Printing 1990.

All rights reserved. No part of this publication may be reproduced, stored in a retrieval system, or trans-
mitted in any form or by any means, mechanical, photocopying, recording, or otherwise, without the prior
written permission of the publisher, Kluwer Academic Publishers, 101 Philip Drive, Assinippi Park, Norwell,
Massachusetts 02061.

Printed in the United States of America

Contents

Contributing Authors

Jerry B. Ayers, Tennessee Technological University

William J. Gephart, Tennessee Technological University

Richard C. Kunkel, National Council for the Accreditation of Teacher Education

Donald M. Medley, University of Virginia

James D. Raths, University of Vermont

Doris L. Redfield, Western Kentucky University

H. Del Schalock, Oregon State System of Higher Education

Nancy L. Zimpher, The Ohio State University

Preface

In an age that dictates accountability and verifiability of educational programs, institutions of higher education are called on to justify their programs. To meet these demands, there is a need for improved methods for the evaluation of teacher education programs. More importantly, there is a need for the development of methods and procedures to conduct continuous and on-going evaluation that can aid the process of program improvement.

Many institutions have had difficulties in developing and implementing satisfactory systems for conducting needed evaluation. In recent years the standards for the approval of teacher education programs in all of the states were strengthened as were the standards for approval by the National Council for the Accreditation of Teacher Education (NCATE). These revised standards put even more emphasis on accountability and the need for both summative and formative evaluation in a teacher education program. Tennessee Technological University has long been recognized as an institution with an exemplary project in program evaluation. As a result, in 1986, the State of Tennessee established at Tennessee Technological University, a Center for Teacher Education Evaluation. The Center began work in July 1986, on the development of models and systems for conducting teacher education program evaluation.

To most, teacher education program evaluation is simple and straightforward. Evaluation includes a set of options, a set of criteria, data collection and interpretation, and then use in meeting accountability needs. Evaluation of teacher education programs is much more. Evaluation can start with two sets of factors including teacher candidate outcomes and K-12 pupil growth goals. At the completion of a teacher education program teacher education candidates should have:

A. Learned the subject matter of a discipline (e.g., physics, history, or elementary education);
B. Mastered the subject matter of general (or liberal) education;
C. Mastered the subject matter of educational theory, history, principles, methods, and techniques of teaching;
D. Performed up to standard in a set of monitored field experiences (e.g., observing teaching, tutoring, and student teaching); and
E. Obtained a provisional license to teach.

After the teacher candidate enters the classroom with a license to teach it is expected that K-12 pupils will:

1. Grow academically;
2. Grow physically, socially, and emotionally;
3. Develop language arts skills;
4. Develop mathematical skills;
5. Learn how to learn; and
6. Become productive members of society.

The explanatory logic for this system is as follows:

IF **X** University's teacher education program is good,
THEN an **X** University teacher education candidate will acquire outcomes A through E.
IF a beginning teacher from **X** University is employed,
THEN K-12 pupils taught by that individual will achieve Goals 1 through 6.

This logic presupposes the outcome. It is desirable to understand how well the program at X University is functioning. How well it is functioning is NOT a given. The logic has another fault. There are two sets of people and two sets of outcomes involved. The learning outcomes of one group of individuals is dependent upon a different set of learning outcomes for the second group.

A more logical set of statements is as follows:

IF teacher candidates acquire A through E
AND their K-12 pupils acquire 1 through 6,
THEN the teacher education program completed by the candidates is good.

This logic falls short since it does not pinpoint specifics of a teacher preparation program in an explanatory way. A through E become a set of proxy variables; however, A through E and 1 through 6 are not identities. How can A through E stand for 1 through 6?

Coupled with the problems noted above are the subtleties and sensitivities of formative and summative evaluation, NCATE Standards, and the issues of accountability. It became obvious early to the staff of the Center for Teacher Education Evaluation that any model or system of teacher education program evaluation needed to have at least six major components, thus the title, "Some Missing Links." In order to assist the staff of the Center in meeting its objectives, it was suggested that there was a need for the assistance from some of the most knowledgeable individuals in the field of teacher education program evaluation.

On May 17-19, 1987, a conference entitled, "Teacher Education Program Evaluation: Some Missing Links," was held in Nashville, Tennessee. Six individuals made presentations about a particular area of teacher education program evaluation and two individuals served in the role of reactors and discussants for the papers. The conference was opened to the higher education community, and 106 individuals from twenty-two states attended and provided comments and reactions to the papers. This volume contains the six papers and comments of the two reactants that were presented as a part of the conference.

In the first paper, H. Del Schalock of the Oregon State System of Higher Education discusssed teacher education candidate selection. Selection of prospective teachers is fundamentally a matter of prediction of success in job performance. The criteria that are now being used in selection and certification of prospective teachers are **weak predictors** of success. There is a chain of entry decisions made by teacher education candidates including: to enter teaching, a college or university, a college or department of education, and a professional preparation program and then to enter the profession through certification, to a teaching position, tenure in a school district, and to enter graduate study. Our inability to make predictions combined with other factors make the task of teacher candidate selection difficult. The purposes of teacher education have not been fully delineated. Certification agencies and commissions control who gets a license to teach, but they never see a candidate teach. Schalock listed other factors that should be of help in candidate selection but are not always used (e.g., knowledge of subject, enabling knowledge, and professional accreditation agencies). Schalock called for increasing the fidelity of predictive measures and sites seven items that hold promise for enhanced predictive power. The paper concluded with five propositions aimed at improving predictive power.

The Executive Director of the National Council for the Accreditation of Teacher Education, Richard C. Kunkel, examined the problems and issues surrounding the evaluation of the education unit. The professional education unit is the college, school, department, or other administrative body within an institution that is officially responsible

for preparation of teachers and other
professional education personnel. Kunkel
perceives the unit as both universal and
particular, minute and encompassing, finite and
bounded, and yet expansive. Education is a
learned profession of which knowledge, skills,
and attitudes are born out of lengthy clinical
experience and a body of knowledge that is
large, incomplete, expanding rapidly, and has
various interpretations. His paper includes
five points that must be considered in an
effective evaluation of a professional
education unit. These include: (1) the unit
as a professional focus (theory and practice),
(2) the impact of the unit focus on other
related agencies, (3) tenants of quality unit
evaluation, (4) accreditation as one form of
unit evaluation, and (5) developing practices
related to programs in the professional unit.
Kunkel terminated his paper with the
recognition that the tasks of evaluation will
not be easy.

James D. Raths of the University of
Vermont addressed the issues related to the
evaluation of teacher education programs. The
paper addresses ways of undertaking a formative
evaluation of a teacher education program.
Raths has grounded his suggestions in a concern
that the evaluation effort be responsive to the
information needs of the persons planning and
delivering the program and also to the need for
specific information about elements in the
program that make it distinctive. A
hypothetical program is described and the
elements of the program were built into the
proposed instrumentation to be used in the
evaluation process. The paper closed with
several cautions about program evaluation.

In the fourth paper, Donald M. Medley of
the University of Virginia examined the issues
related to outcomes assessment. Outcomes-based
teacher preparation should be a component of
any teacher education program along with
general education, courses on didactics, and an
organized, full set of "field studies." The
preparation program should be a continuous

series of exercises designed to assess the
teacher candidate's reaction and responses to
teaching problems arranged to simulate a normal
day of teaching. Medley focused on a four by
four matrix of problem classes. Each of the
sixteen cells would contain classes of common
problems. A teacher candidate should learn to
respond to the various sets of problems with
some degree of consistency. Each teacher over
the course should develop a "personal theory"
of teaching. Given such a personal theory, the
teacher in training should have a structure on
which to hang the solutions of instructional
problem solving. The person who fails to
develop such a theory would be expected to
respond erratically to the individual and
classes of problems. Medley discussed the
general procedures for developing outcome-based
teacher preparation programs.

Jerry B. Ayers, Director of the Center for
Teacher Education Evaluation at Tennessee
Technological University, presented a
discussion of the issues and problems related
to follow-up evaluation. Follow-up evaluation
was and continues to be a major problem for
institutions seeking accreditation. The
redesigned NCATE Standards that became
effective for institutions seeking
accreditation after 1986-87 put extensive
emphases on all types of evaluation and, in
particular, follow-up evaluation of graduates
after they enter the profession. Follow-up
evaluation must be systematic and involve
observation in the classrooms of the graduates.
The paper included suggestions for beginning
the design of a follow-up study, conducting
follow-up evaluation, and using the results for
program improvement.

The sixth paper, by Doris L. Redfield of
Western Kentucky University, examined the
weakest link in the total process of program
evaluation, that is, the relationship of pupil
achievement to the preparation program of the
teacher. At best, measurers of pupil
achievement may provide indirect indicators of
teaching performance. Pupil achievement may be

necessary but insufficient for demonstrating teaching effectiveness. Considerations that are important to defining pupil achievement and its role in the evaluation of teaching include: purpose of the evaluation, intended evaluation targets, and components of those targets. Sophisticated statistical techniques, such as regression modeling, may need to be set aside temporarily so as not to drive the development of appropriate evaluation systems. In developing appropriate evaluation systems, it is important to consider that there may not be one best set of pupil achievement or teaching effectiveness indicators. Program effectiveness is very much context specific.

In the last two papers, Nancy L. Zimpher and William J. Gephart, respectively, summarized various aspects of the conference and present ideas for the future. Zimpher provided an analysis of the conference themes and concerns for the future. Gephart elaborted further on the missing links of teacher education program evaluation.

It is hoped that this book will be useful in helping solve the problems related to teacher education evaluation. The staff of the Center for Teacher Education Evaluation is developing a model for teacher education evaluation based on the accreditation process. This model will be of use to institutions in meeting accountability needs, accreditation standards and, most importantly, in improving their programs for the preparation of teachers.

Acknowledgements

We would like to acknowledge a number of individuals and agencies who contributed to the development of this publication. To Nancy L. Zimpher, thank you for encouraging the Center for Teacher Education Evaluation to conduct a conference in the Spring of 1987 that led to this publication. To the authors of the articles, thank you for sharing your expert opinions and insights about the evaluation of teacher education programs. To the persons who attended the conference "Teacher Education Evaluation: Some Missing Links," thank you for your time and comments.

We appreciate the financial support for the Conference derived from a grant to Tennessee Technological University from the Centers of Excellence program of the Tennessee Higher Education Commission. Also, we would like to thank Mr. W. A. Goodwin, Associate Vice President for Research at Tennessee Technological University for the additional financial assistance provided through his office.

Thank you to the individuals, in particular, Oneida L. Martin, Assistant Professor of Education, who contributed to this book by making the Spring 1987 Conference a success. Thank you to those who were involved in the editing, word processing, and sorting and collating the many pieces of paper associated with this undertaking. Without the efforts of Joy Johns, Editorial Consultant; Diann Walker, Secretary; Sandra D. Miles (who prepared the final copy for all of the figures), Anita C. Odle, and Patricia A. Stanton, graduate assistants in the Center for Teacher Education Evaluation; and Sharon A. Heard, Patricia A. Eaves, and Edith Young, support staff in the College of Education this publication would not have been possible.

Finally, at the personal level, thank you to our wives, Ginny Gephart and Mary N. Ayers, for their support, patience and understanding.

1

TEACHER SELECTION: A PROBLEM OF ADMISSION CRITERIA, CERTIFICATION CRITERIA,OR PREDICTION OF JOB PERFORMANCE?

H. Del Schalock
Oregon State System of Higher Education

SYNOPSIS

The selection of prospective teachers should be a matter of predicting success on the job, but at present selection is according to other criteria. The criteria currently used in selecting and certifying teachers do not predict job performance and, therefore, need to be reviewed and strengthened immediately.

The purpose of the paper is to explore the rationale underlying these views, and trace their implications in the teacher selection process.

CURRENT STATUS OF TEACHER SELECTION

The 1987 March-April issue of the **Journal of Teacher Education** is devoted to preservice teacher selection and retention and, therefore, provides a good foundation to the present paper. Applegate's article (1987) is useful because she provides a succinct overview of recent literature in the area. A number of key

issues are addressed for consideration when
trying to understand the nature and purpose of
admission/retention criteria in the context of
teacher education. Other recent publications
that add significantly to the literature on
teacher selection are the chapter by Howey in
The Education of Teachers: A Look Ahead (Howey
and Gardener, Eds., 1983, see especially pp.
28-36.); the chapter by Howey and Strom in
Advances in Teacher Education (Haberman and
Backus, Eds., 1987); and the chapter by
Schwartz in **The Dynamics of Change In Teacher
Education, Vol. I.** (Lashley, Ed, 1987).

Applegate's discussion of the purpose of
teacher selection and the standards and
criteria used in making selection decisions are
both timely and insightful in light of the
many national reports now calling for the
improvement of teacher quality. She argues
that "selection is a form of evaluating an
individual's capacity or potential to be
successful at a task" (p. 2), but in the
selection of teachers we are not at all clear
about the task for which we are evaluating. In
part this is because the development of a
teacher is a lengthy and complex process, and

> . . . the view of selection must be
> broad enough to reflect developmental
> considerations. Individuals who hope
> to have teaching as a career face
> several decisions and review points:
> entry into a college or university,
> entry into a college or department of
> education, entry into a professional
> preparation program, entry into the
> profession of teaching through
> certification, entry into a teaching
> position, entry into graduate study,
> and tenure in a school district. Each
> of these phases of preparation for a
> teaching career has a different
> purpose and, thus, could have
> different selective admission
> requirements (p. 3).

From the perspective of the present paper, however, and from Applegate's perspective as well, this multifaceted process is only one of the reasons why we are unclear about the focus of evaluation in teacher selection. The other is that "teacher educators have not successfully defined the purpose of teacher education" (Applegate, p.3). Obviously, the mission of teacher preparation programs is to identify and prepare effective teachers, but little consensus exists on what an effective teacher means. There is even less agreement on what effective teaching means under various conditions of teaching, for example, teaching in an inner city versus a rural school, an elementary versus a secondary school, a school emphasizing cooperative learning versus individually guided instruction, or a school emphasizing goal-based mastery learning versus textbook-based normative learning (Howey and Strom, 1987). Schalock (1987) has called this **the problem of context.** Attempting to assure quality in the graduates of teacher preparation programs is equally as pressing as attempting to define effective teaching or to predict the effectiveness of a particular teacher in a particular job setting.

While teacher educators have been remiss in clarifying the purpose of teacher education, teacher certification agencies have done little to help. Traditionally certification has depended upon the successful completion of a prescribed course of study registered by a transcript of course titles, grades and a summative evaluation of performance in student teaching. The prescribed coursework is assumed to cover the knowledge and skills that teachers need to be effective, and performance in student teaching is assumed to be a good indicator or predictor of the ability of a prospective teacher to transfer his/her knowledge and skills into practice. However, teacher certification agencies rarely demand evidence of the candidate's effectiveness as a teacher. No certifying agency in the nation, for example, currently requires proof that a teacher candidate is able to foster learning in the students they teach! The rapid spread of teacher testing as part of the admission/certification process has added to the confusion surrounding the issue of evaluative criteria in teacher selection. In one regard, teacher testing has highlighted the need for clearly stated, objective criteria for entry into the profession. On the other hand, it has focused on teacher attributes that are **assumed** to be related to effective teaching. Skill mastery and knowledge of content are undoubtedly necessary for a teacher to be effective, but they in no way assure competence; nor does the demonstration of particular teaching behaviors. By focusing on teacher knowledge and skills rather than on the performance of job related responsibilities, certifying agencies have not forced teacher education faculties or the profession at large to deal with the bottom line issues surrounding teacher selection. These agencies need to consider the teacher's ability to manage classrooms as contexts for learning or a teacher's ability to accomplish learning gains in "hard-to-teach" students.

In fairness to teacher education faculties and certifying agencies, it should be pointed out that professional associations and national accreditiing agencies need to help clarify these bottom line issues. Such is also the case with most state and national reports associated with the improvement of teachers and teaching. Both AACTE and NCATE, for example, focus on the content and organization of preparation programs rather than the selection and performance of individual candidates. The reports by the Holmes Group (1986) and the National Commission for Excellence in Teacher Education (1985) also deliberate these issues.

Two exceptions to this traditional focus on programs are the reports by the Carnegie Task Force on Teaching as a Profession (1986) and the Southern Regional Education Board (1985). In both cases these reports consider the ability of teachers to foster learning in

students or teacher productivity as the primary
criteria for teacher selection. This example
represents a radical departure in thinking
about teacher selection and, if practiced, may
send shock waves through the profession, making
the response to current teacher testing
practices look like a modest tremor.

Proposition I. Teacher Selection Is Fundamentally A Matter of Prediction

Teacher selection is fundamentally a matter of
predicting the success of a candidate as a
teacher. Success in teaching should be
defined primarily in terms of pupil learning.
This is an "output" definition of teacher
effectiveness, rather than a "process"
definition, and aligns with the recommendations
of the Carnegie Task Force on Teaching and the
Southern Regional Education Board.

This view does not deny the importance of
assessing the knowledge and skills posssessed
by teacher candidates as part of the selection
process, nor does it deny the importance of
assessing background experience, personal
traits and interpersonal relationships with
pupils and colleagues. It does not even deny
the importance of grade-point averages, SAT or
ACT scores. This view does argue, however,
that the legitimacy of such measures comes only
if they are viewed as **potential predictors** of
success in teaching, success being defined
primarily in terms of ability to foster pupil
learning. To rely upon enabling knowledge,
skills or traits, as something more than they
are, or even to view them as potential
predictors without an accompanying research
designed to determine their utility is to beg
issue imbedded in the task of teacher
selection.

Teacher selection has as its purpose the
identification of teacher candidates who have a
high probability of success in accomplishing
the kind of learning outcomes in pupils that
are desired by the state and/or community in

which a teacher is hired. Within this frame of reference the measures and criteria used in the selection process need to be valid and reliable predictors of the candidate's ability to accomplish particular kinds of learning goals with certain kinds of learners in specific kinds of school settings. Anything less causes the teacher selection process to be less than it should.

Proposition II. At This Point In Time We Do Not Have Strong Predictors of Success In Teaching

Nearly a decade ago (Schalock, 1979) I completed an analysis of the available research on teacher effectiveness from the perspective of teacher selection. The purpose of the review was both practical and theoretical. As a teacher educator I sought to identify measures that could be used in the teacher selection process as reliable predictors of teacher effectiveness. As a researcher I sought to establish a framework for thinking about the prediction of teacher effectiveness. I also wished to include a way of ordering the research literature related to the ability to predict who might or might not be effective as a teacher.

The framework that emerged from this work was organized around the concept of the **fidelity** of predictive measures. The concept of fidelity deals with the extent to which a predictive measure is similar or "isomorphic" to the behavior that is to be predicted. Examples of high fidelity predictors in teacher selection research are samples taken during actual teaching conditions and teaching under simplified classroom conditions; examples of low fidelity predictors are measures of personality and attitudes toward teaching. Knowledge of subject matter to be taught and performance during simulated teaching conditions, such as micro-teaching, fall somewhere in between. Imbedded in the construct is the hypothesis that the higher the fidelity of a measure, the better it should be as a predictor (Schalock, 1979, p. 369).

Seven broad categories of variables were identified that held potential as predictors of teaching effectiveness. Ordered according to their expected predictive power these were:

1. Work samples, for example, the teaching of lessons or a unit of study with attention being given to pupil learning;
2. The ability to engage students in learning activities;
3. The ability to perform the functions required of teachers;
4. Skills related to teaching;
5. Knowledge related to teaching;
6. Experience with children and youth; and
7. Intelligence and academic ability.

Given recent developments in teacher testing, an eighth category would now need to be added. This category would rank in terms of its potential as a predictor of teaching effectiveness: mastery of basic skills.

A reasonably exhaustive review of the research available then concerning each of these broad categories of predictors yielded disappointing results. Some categories indicated that the first three categories were in fact better predictors than the next four, but predictive relationships or correlations within any category were consistently small or inconsistent. Essentially no relationship was found to exist between school-based measures of effectiveness in teaching and a prospective teacher's experience with children or mastery of knowledge related to teaching. The overall conclusion drawn from the research available at the time was that ". . . research on teacher effectiveness has little to contribute to decisions about who should enter the teaching profession." (Schalock, 1979, pp. 407-408).[1]

Generally, research that has occurred within the past decade does not alter this conclusion. Little formal research has been done on the first three categories of predictors, and no startling breakthroughs have occurred on the last four. Some progress has been made in sorting out the relationship that exists between mastery of content to be taught (as measured by NTE examinations) and success in teaching advanced courses in subject areas. Little else in the overall picture has changed; especially no new evidence concerning enhanced predictive power has emerged. The sad truth seems to be that while the literature reviewed in the **Third Handbook of Research on Teaching** (Wittrock, 1986) has increased in both quality and volume, we are essentially without any reliable predictors of who will or will not be good teachers.

What has changed in the last decade is a growing appreciation of the power of context as a determiner of teacher effectiveness. Some indication of this surfaced in the 1978 review. For example, the repeated finding in Oregon College of Education studies (now Western Oregon State College) was that the judged complexity/difficulty of a teaching context predicated more accurately the effectiveness of student teachers and first-year teachers than any other predictive measure used. The

---

[1]It should be pointed out that without exception the measures of teacher effectiveness used in the studies reviewed were weak (this included measures relying on Standardized tests of achievement). The predictive relationships expected within the analytic framework may begin to surface when stronger dependent measures are used, for example, criterion referenced tests that are aligned with the curriculum being taught.

research in the Beginning Teacher Evaluation Study (BTSE) found that what teachers did to foster learning in students varied appreciably across subject areas at the same grade level and across grade levels in the same subject area. This sensitivity to context effects appears repeatedly in the **Third Handbook** (see for example, pp. 397, 515 and 587), and the preliminary findings in the BTES study have been verified and extended through a recent study by Lara and Medley (1987). Using three different observation schedules these authors found that teaching behavior that fostered learning in students not only varied by grade level and subject area but also by high and low-ability students within grades and subjects as well.

Given what we now know about the interdependence of context and teacher effectiveness, the prediction of teacher effectiveness obviously has to take the matter of context into account. So do teacher education programs hoping to assure certifying agencies or hiring districts that their graduates will be effective teachers.

Dealing with the problem of context when predicting the effectiveness of teachers. How is it possible for a teacher preparation institution to give assurances to a certifying agency or hiring district that a graduate will be effective as a teacher without knowing in advance who is to be taught, what is to be taught, or the conditions under which teaching is to occur? This discussion draws heavily from an article recently published in the **Journal of Teacher Education** entitled "The Central Issue in Teacher Warranties: Quality Assurance for What?" (Schalock, 1987).

How can teacher education programs be designed to prepare students to deal effectively with variations in context when teaching? To be effective, teachers must vary their

instructional plans and procedures to
accommodate not only differences in students,
but differences in subject matter, learning
goals within a subject area, the instructional
resources that are available, the available
time for teaching, and other extraneous
variables. These preparations require teachers
to use decision making processes aimed at
searching for applications among these various
instructional contexts, their knowledge of the
subject and their repertoire of apparent
instructional strategies and procedures.
(Doyle, 1986; Corno and Snow, 1986). As Brophy
and Evertson (1976, p. 139) stated more than a
decade ago,

> Effective teaching is not simply a
> matter of implementing a small number
> of basic skills. Instead, effective
> teaching requires the ability to
> implement a very large number of
> diagnostic, instructional, managerial,
> and therapeutic skills, tailoring
> behavior in specific contexts and
> situations to the specific needs of
> the moment. Effective teachers not
> only must be able to do a large number
> of things; they also must be able to
> recognize which of the many things
> they know how to do applies at the
> given moment and be able to follow
> through by performing the behavior
> effectively.

If this is an accurate picture of what an
effective teacher must do, how does a teacher
preparation institution equip its graduates to
function in this manner? To do so surely
involves more than providing students with
relatively isolated sets of teaching skills
(i.e., general methods), more than some
background knowledge about human development
and learning (i.e., foundations) and certainly
more than a work out in teaching the subject
areas (i.e., content mastery and special
methods). If practicing teachers are, above

all else, decision makers searching for the optimum condition among methods, materials, learning goals, student characteristics and other variables, then surely students of teaching need to have extensive training and guidance in the practice of such decision making. Further, to help establish the effectiveness of teacher candidates, candidates need to demonstrate their ability to make decisions; this performance must weighed against some standard that indicates an acceptable or unacceptable level of accomplishment. Deciding how best to prepare teacher candidates through a politically and economically feasible program is an issue that has to be resolved by any teacher education institution hoping to engage in prediction studies or to assure the probable success of its graduates in particular job settings.

To what extent do context effects need to be controlled measures of teacher performance and how is this to be done? If performance is always influenced by context, it would seem important to control or identify these effects when obtaining measures of teaching performance that are used for prediction or quality control. One approach is to have prospective teachers demonstrate their ability to teach in situations that are reasonably similar to all classroom situations. Microteaching and other forms of simulated or laboratory teaching environment make this possible. However, if teaching performance is assessed in an ongoing classroom, it is a difficult procedure. In school settings, children, instructional resources, goals for learning, support and assistance from supervisors, and school and community environments, vary appreciably for each practicum or student teacher placement. This poses a dilemma for teacher preparation institutions, which must decide whether to submit to a more stringentbut less valid measure of teaching effectiveness (and probably a less powerful predictor of teacher

12

effectiveness) in order to control context
effects; or to accept a more liberal approach
to measurement in order to obtain contextual
validity. (For a related discussion of the
importance of contextual validity in
educational measurement, see Shulman, 1970.)

**How can performance in a specialized
educational setting be generalized to unknown
settings?** In the best conditions relatively few
in-depth evaluations can be made of the
performance of teacher candidates in ongoing
school settings during the course of a
preparation program. Teaching practicum
experiences typically limit opportunities for
such evaluations, and student teaching
placements typically provide only two or three
weeks of independent, full-time teaching. This
poses two dilemmas for institutions that hope
to predict/assure the quality of their
graduates. One is the problem of generalizing
from a limited number of performance samples.
The other problem is generalizing teaching
contexts that will vary significantly from the
context in which teaching performance has been
observed. Short of totally restructuring the
way in which teacher education is carried out
in the United States, can this dilemma be
overcome? If it cannot, can the prediction of
teacher effectiveness or the assurance of
quality in graduates ever be realized?

**How are teacher education programs to connect
functionally to instructional models and
programs in the schools?** Historically, teacher
education programs have been designed with
little attention to programs in the schools.
Some attention usually is given to state-
required curricula, but far greater attention
tends to be given to human development and
learning, theory and methods of teaching,
research on effective teaching and effective
schools, and other aspects of educational
foundations. Attention also tends to be given

to national trends in education, national curriculum projects, national or state laws pertaining to education and, in recent years, to the application of computers and other forms of high technology in education. Beyond curriculum requirements, however, state or local approaches to schooling tend to have minor impact on either the content or the design of teacher preparation programs.

This traditional lack of local orientation in teacher education stems from a number of factors. The obligation of a teacher education faculty is to prepare students for a wide range of school environments since no one can anticipate where graduates of a particular program will be hired to work. Additionally, teacher education faculty tend to be eclectic in their preference for models of schooling and to take the view that their obligation is to expose rather than to propose.

Still another factor has been the absence of clear-cut models of schooling at the state or local levels. Until recently, few states or districts have been actively involved in designing alternative approaches to schooling or in adopting an approach to schooling as the model to be implemented. This latter condition is no longer the case, and it has major implications for institutions that prepare teachers. States and districts around the nation have or are launching major efforts to improve their schools. Moreover, in nearly all cases, the approaches to school improvement adopted by districts and states reflect the growing knowledge concerning effective teaching and effective schools. This concern calls for teaching practices that are not addressed by teacher preparation institutions. If teacher education institutions are geared to improve education, they should be preparing teachers to operate within the guidelines that are adopted in their state or geographic region.

How do teacher preparation institutions that wish to predict or assure the effectiveness of their graduates approach this kind of mismatch? At a recent Wingspread conference on teacher warranties (Barr and Schalock, 1986) Dr. Gary Griffin, Dean of the School of Education, University of Illinois-Chicago, suggested that this could be accomplished best by forming a coalition or "compact" between a teacher preparation institution and a network of participating school districts in order to design and operate teacher preparation programs. Dr. Phillip Schlechty, Director of the Gheens Professional Development Academy of the Jefferson County Public Schools-Louisville, argued at the same conference that this mismatch may never be resolved. Consequently, teacher preparation institutions should assume responsibility only for graduates who will learn how to teach rather than know how to teach. While such a stance would surely simplify the issues that have been discussed here, it would not simplify the overriding and long-term issue of assuring quality in the teacher workforce.

Proposition III. As a Responsible Party in the Selection of Teachers, Preparation Institutions Should Seek Powerful Predictors of Success in Teaching

If teacher selection is basically a matter of prediction, then teacher preparation institutions should search for and use the most powerful preditors available of success in teaching. The research literature is not particularly helpful in this regard, but the conceptual framework outlined earlier should serve as a useful place to begin. Figure 1 translates this framework into a chart that may have clearer meaning for the teacher educator desiring to make these necessary and urgent predictions.

A measurement/prediction scheme can be translated into an operational teacher preparation program. Designing a program with concurring evidence and performance standards to recommend a candidate for certification will not only clarify issues of measurement, but

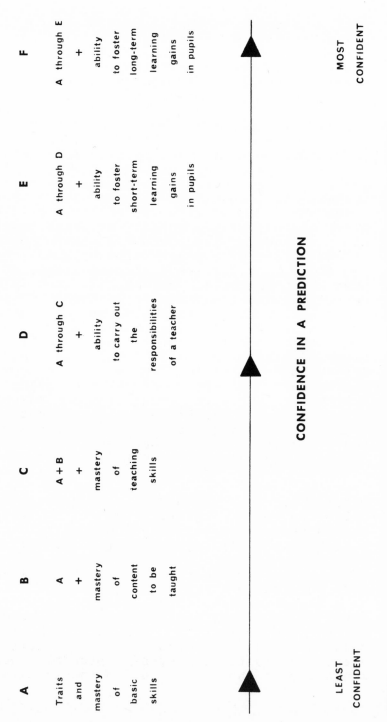

KIND AND LEVEL OF EVIDENCE

A	B	C	D	E	F
Traits and mastery of basic skills	A + mastery of content to be taught	A + B + mastery of teaching skills	A through C + ability to carry out the responsibilities of a teacher	A through D + ability to foster short-term learning gains in pupils	A through E + ability to foster long-term learning gains in pupils

CONFIDENCE IN A PREDICTION

LEAST CONFIDENT

MOST CONFIDENT

FIGURE 1. A FRAMEWORK FOR THINKING ABOUT THE POWER OF PREDICTIVE MEASURES.

will also elucidate the content and
organization of the instructional program.
Evidence may be desired of a candidate's
ability to foster learning in both slow and
fast learning students and in concept and skill
learning in more than one subject area. Clear
implications, then, exist for what is to be
learned and practiced by a candidate prior to
student teaching.

Additionally, an institution needs to
check the accuracy of its predictions of
quality assurance in teacher education.
Ideally this should be done as part of a long-
range program of research on the predictive
power of the various quality assurance measures
and standards used and generally on the
effectiveness of a preparation program. Short
of this, the follow-up studies required for
program approval by NCATE and state
certification agencies can be used. Without
some effort to obtain follow-up information on
the accuracy of predictions about graduates,
however, the concept of teacher selection as a
form of prediction holds little meaning. It
also holds little value as a program
improvement strategy or as a means for
extending knowledge about teacher education.
The design of teacher education programs as
contexts for research has been discussed at
some length by Schalock & Girod (1975),
Schalock (1979) and Schalock (1983).

**Proposition IV. As a Responsible Party In the
Selection of Teachers, Certifying Agencies
Should Demand Increasingly Powerful Evidence of
a Candidate's Effectiveness As a Teacher**

If teacher preparation institutions move to
more powerful measures of teaching performance
as a basis for candidates being recommended for
certification, certifying agencies should move
in the same direction. In fact, they should
take the lead in this movement. Certification
agencies need to act beyond a program approval
mentality in their gatekeeping function for the

profession. Their decisions about certification must be anchored in hard evidence concerning the performance capabilities of each teacher candidate. This should include defensible evidence that a candidate is in fact able to accomplish a variety of learning goals when working with different types of learners in various instructional settings. Anything less than this provides a weak basis for certification regardless of what a candidate may know or be able to do.

Proposition V. As a Responsible Party In the Selection of Teachers, Hiring Districts Should Demand Increasingly Powerful Evidence of an Applicant's Effectiveness As a Teacher

The last defense of assuring quality in the teaching workforce, at least as the profession is now structured, rests with the hiring and performance evaluation practices of local districts. These are notoriously uneven, and at the present time provide an unknown degree of protection against teacher incompetence, but they are the best we have. Increasing attention is being directed to both the importance and the process of teacher evaluation (e.g., the April, 1987 issue of **Educational Leadership**) and the staff development programs needed to accompany a functional evaluation system. Much, however, remains to be done. Figure 2 conveys in schematic form the critical role that district hiring and evaluation practices play in assuring quality in the teaching workforce. The concept of tenure, equivalent to a million dollar decision by a local district, helps convey the importance of this decision locally.

PROJECTIONS FOR THE YEARS AHEAD

Catherine Cornbleth's recent article entitled "Ritual and Rationality in Teacher Education Reform" (Cornbleth, 1986) provides an

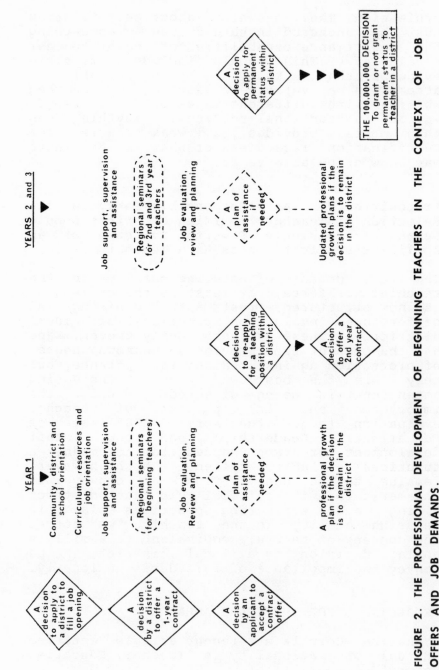

YEAR 1

Community, district and school orientation

Curriculum, resources and job orientation

Job support, supervision and assistance

Regional seminars for beginning teachers

Job evaluation, Review and planning

A plan of assistance if needed

A professional growth plan if the decision is to remain in the district

A decision to apply to a district to fill a job opening

A decision by a district to offer a 1-year contract

A decision by an applicant to accept a contract offer

YEARS 2 and 3

Job support, supervision and assistance

Regional seminars for 2nd and 3rd year teachers

Job evaluation, review and planning

A plan of assistance if needed

Updated professional growth plans if the decision is to remain in the district

A decision to re-apply for a teaching position within a district

A decision to offer a 2nd year contract

A decision to apply for permanent status within a district

THE 100,000,000 DECISION To grant or not grant permanent status to teacher in a district

FIGURE 2. THE PROFESSIONAL DEVELOPMENT OF BEGINNING TEACHERS IN THE CONTEXT OF JOB OFFERS AND JOB DEMANDS.

appropriate model for projections about the future. She argues that "....how we see, think and talk about, study, and act on matters of teacher education and schooling" (p. 9) shape our discussion of problems and plausible solutions. She further argues that the aim of state and national reports calling for reform are reestablishing the support of school personnel preparation, which is (1984) characterized as "an expressive activity of pomp and circumstance...a dance of legitimacy, not a strategy of change" (p. 128).

The thesis and related propositions advanced here go a long way toward changing how we see, think, talk about, study, and act on matters concerning teacher education and schooling. They are designed to move the current discussion of reform beyond the structure of teacher preparation, beyond the length of training and beyond the content included in teacher preparation programs; they are structured to focus on the issue of a teacher's ability to nurture student learning.

I would predict that an uncompromising and unrelenting focus on student learning will generate the kinds of change in schooling and the preparation of school personnel that Cornbleth doubts will ever occur. This focus must be acknowledged by teacher candidates, college supervisors of teacher candidates, school supervisors of teacher candidates, the institution recommending a candidate for certification, the agency granting a certificate, the district that hiring a teacher, and the district granting permanent status to a teacher.

REFERENCES

Applegate, J. A. (1987). Teacher candidate selection: An overview. **Journal of Teacher Education**, 38(2), 2-6.

Barr, R. D. & Schalock, H. D. (1986). **Quality assurance in teacher education.** A summary report of a Wingspread conference. Oregon State University – Western Oregon State College School of Education, Corvallis, OR.

Brophy, J. E., & Everston, D. M. (1976). **Learning from teaching: A developmental perspective.** Boston: Allyn & Bacon.

Carnegie Task Force on Teaching as a Profession. (1986). **A nation prepared: teachers for the twenty-first century.** New York: Carnegie Forum on Education and the Economy.

Cornbleth, C. (1986, April). Ritual and rationality in teacher education reform. **Educational Researcher, 15,** 5-14.

Corno, L., & Snow, R. E. (1986). Adapting teaching to individual differences among learners. In M. C. Wittrock (Ed.), **Third handbook of research on teaching** (pp. 605-629). New York: Macmillan.

Deal, T. E. (1984). Educational change: Revival tent, tinkertoys, jungle or carnival? **Teachers College Record, 86(1),** 124-137.

Doyle, W. (1986). Classroom organization and management. In M. C. Wittrock (Ed.), **Third Handbook of research on teaching** (pp. 392-431). New York: Macmillan.

Educational Leadership (1987), **44(7),** pp 3-75.

Howey, K. R. (1983). Teacher education: An overview. In K. Howey and W. Gardner (eds.), **The education of teachers: A look ahead** (pp 6-37). New York: Longman.

Howey, K. R. & Strom, S. M. (1987). Teacher selection reconsidered. In M. Haberman and J. Backus (Eds.), **Advances in Teacher Education III,** (pp 1-34). Norwood, NJ: Ablex.

Journal of Teacher Education (1987), **38(2),** 2-30.

Lara, A. V., & Medley, D. M. (1987). Effective teacher behavior as a function of learner ability. **Professional School Psychology,** 2(1), 15-33.

National Commission for Excellence in Teacher
    Education. (1985). **A call for change in
    teacher education.** Washington: American
    Association of Colleges for Teacher
    Education.
Schalock, H. D. (1979). Research on teacher
    selection. In D. C. Berliner (Ed.),
    Annual review of research in education
    (pp. 364-417). Washington: American
    Educational Research Association.
Schalock, H. D. (1987). Methodological
    considerations in future research and
    development in teacher education. In K.
    Howey & W. Gardner (Eds.), **The education
    of teachers: a look ahead** (pp 38-73). New
    York: Longman.
Schalock, H. D. (1987). The central issue in
    teacher warranties: quality assurance for
    what? **Journal of Teacher Education,
    38**(5), 52-58.
Schalock, H. D. and Girod, G. R. (1975). The
    Oregon College of Education-Teaching
    Research Division. Paragigm for research
    on teacher preparation. In G. E. Dickson,
    Ed., **Research and evaluation in
    operational competency-based teacher
    education programs.** College of Education,
    University of Toledo, No. 1., 21-38.
Schwartz, H. (1986). Recruitment, selection,
    retention and graduation of teacher
    education candidates. In T. Lasley (Ed.),
    **The dynamics of change in teacher
    education: Volume I** (pp. 29-43).
    Washington: American Association of
    Colleges for Teacher Education.
Shulman, L. S. (1970). Reconstruction in
    educational research. **Review of
    Educational Research, 40,** 371-396.
The Holmes Group. (1986). **Tomorrow's
    teachers: a report of the Holmes Group.**
    East Lansing, MI: The Holmes Group.
Wittrock, M. C. (Ed.), (1986). **Third handbook
    of research on teaching.** New York:
    Macmillan.

ABOUT THE AUTHOR

H. Del Schalock is Research Professor in the
Teaching Research Division, Oregon State System
of Higher Education and Assistant Dean for
Research and Development, Oregon State
University-Western Oregon State College School
of Education. Previously he held teaching and
research positions at Oklahoma State University
and Oregon State University. He received the
Ph.D. in Educational Psychology and Measurement
from the University of Nebraska and completed
post doctoral work at the Merrill-Palmer
Institute in Detroit and the Tavistock Clinic
in London. He has published over seventy-five
articles in a variety of publications and has
published chapters in twelve books. His
current research interests are in goal-based
instructional programs in elementary and
secondary schools, teacher supervision/
evaluation systems that take pupil learning
into account, and continuing professional
development programs for school personnel that
lead to school improvement.

2

EVALUATION OF TEACHER EDUCATION PROGRAMS

James D. Raths
University of Vermont

INTRODUCTION

Our task is to advance a plan for carrying out
a formative evaluation of a teacher education
program. Since the plan is to be specific and
precise, a concrete case should be adopted,
such as a program in elementary education at
the University of Florida, circa 1974. Even
though the program was planned more than
fifteen years ago, it could be planned to meet
NCATE's new standards of curriculum design,
Standard 1A, "based on a formally adopted
professional model that explicates the
purposes, processes, outcomes, and evaluation
of each program area. The rationale (for the
model and the knowledge bases that undergird
them) is clearly stated along with the goals,
philosophy and objectives for the program."
(NCATE, 1986, p. 26).

THE OBJECT OF THE EVALUATION

The program at the University of Florida is based on Comb's (1965, p. 20) conception of teaching as a helping profession, and it addresses the following goals:

1. To strengthen the rich and extensive perceptions each candidate has about his/her subject field,
2. To improve the accuracy of perceptions candidates have about what people are like,
3. To advance candidates' perceptions of self that lead to adequacy in the teaching role,
4. To improve the accuracy of perceptions candidates have about the purposes and processes of learning, and
5. To enrich and broaden personal perceptions about the appropriate methods for carrying out his/her instructional purposes.

The program is committed as well to what Gideonse called "clinical fidelity", meaning that the program is offered in a manner consistent with its own goals. In sum, this commitment is a reflection of NCATE's Standard 1B., Delivery of the Curriculum. (NCATE, 1986, p. 27). To this end, the program is based on the following principles:

1. People behave according to choices they make from among alternatives they see available to them at the moment.
2. It is more appropriate for people to learn a few concepts rather than many facts.
3. Learning is much more efficient if the learner feels a need to know that which is being learned.
4. Learning has two aspects: (a) acquiring new information and (b) discovering the personal meaning of that informtion.
5. No one specific item of information and no specific skill is essential for effective teaching.

6. People learn more easily and rapidly if they help make the important decisions about their learning.
7. People learn and grow more quickly if they are not afraid to make mistakes.
8. Objectivity is not a valuable asset for a teacher. What is needed instead is a concern for students.
9. Teachers teach the way they have been taught, not the way they have been taught to teach.
10. Pressure on students produces negative behaviors such as cheating, avoidance, fearfulness, etc.
11. Teachers are more effective as their mental health improves, thus freeing creativity, self-motivation, and concern for others.

The program is delivered through three major components--the seminar, the substantive panel, and the field experience.

A professor delivers the seminar, and he is assigned a group of thirty candidates for the duration of the two-year sequence of professional education. The candidates range from beginners to those just about to graduate. As candidates complete the program, replacements are added to the group.

The thirty candidates are divided into two groups for discussion purposes. The discussion groups meet two hours a week--often in informal settings such as faculty homes or in candidates' rooms. To enhance group cohesiveness, all thirty candidates also meet once a week and gather together informally on other occasions during the semester.

The seminar is the place where, through discussion and exploration, the candidates discover the personal meaning of the learnings and experiences they are acquiring in other phases of the program. Individual records are maintained on each candidate in the seminar. The records include diaries kept by the candidates, describing their experiences and activities in the program and evaluations of their progress by members of the teacher

education faculty. The instructor of the
seminar also distributes a weekly newsletter.
While seminar instructors vary in their
approaches, all attempts to help the candidates
focus on their own self-development. Some use
standard exercises that are derivative of the
"human potential" movement of the 1960's.
Examples include role playing exercises and
group problem solving tasks. Candidates are
asked to take strong positions on various
issues and to share with others their
understandings of the origin of their beliefs.
Other instructors do not introduce such
procedures but merely invite candidates to
share their experiences. As topics are
introduced in this informal setting, the
instructors engage candidates in a search for
personal meanings.

A second component of the University of
Florida program is the substantive panel. This
panel is made up of faculty members who usually
teach methods, curriculum, and foundations
courses. Instead of convening classes, panel
members prepare and distribute a list of
learning activities that candidates are to
complete. Included in the list are some
activities required of all candidates, but a
large number are optional, and candidates are
encouraged to propose their own activities if
they are convinced a substitute is desirable.
The first required activity is to attend an
orientation session in which the entire package
of activities for a given area (e.g., reading
methods, the philosophy of education, etc.) is
introduced.

The third component of the program is
field experience, which is a continuous part of
the program. Candidates actively engage in
some responsible roles in school during each
semester of the program. As with other
segments of the program, the evaluations of
candidate progress in field experiences are
recorded on appropriate forms and filed with
the seminar leader. These evaluations are
collated with others generated by the
candidates' efforts and used in the seminars to

help candidates perceive more accurately the progress they are making.

Summative evaluations of candidate progress are rendered by a committee of professors, teaching assistants, and cooperating teachers. The panel reviews the pertinent artifacts included in each candidate's portfolio and the evaluations submitted by instructors in all three components of the program. Judgments are not characterized in the form of traditional grades; instead, a pass/no pass option is used. A candidate who does not pass the criteria has the option of repeating the program.

EVALUATION AS A PROBLEMATIC ENTERPRISE

There are many program evaluation models extant, some generic (Brandt, 1981), and some specific to teacher education. (Nelli and Nutter, 1984). The goals of this program and its proposed modus operandi are clearer, perhaps, than those found in most programs. We need to propose a formative evaluation of this teacher education program at the University of Florida because there are some problems with it.

The thrust of formative evaluation is to ask the question, " Are we doing it right?" (Summative evaluation asks, "Are we right in doing it?") The point of addressing the formative question is that when the findings suggest that the program, for whatever reason, is "not being done right" or implemented in ways congruent with the adopted program design, then interventions designed to get the program centered again should be considered. Yet, so often, even when data are generated in an evaluation which gives credence to the claim that the program is weak, is rated poorly by its candidates, or discredited by external evaluators, very little is done with the results. Katz, et al. (1981) suggest at least several problems with formative evaluation

designs that hinder their usefulness and
relevance. Their list of problems includes the
credibility of the data included in the report,
the verisimilitude of the findings, and the
focus of the recommendations. While all of
these elements are relevant to carrying out
formative evaluations, the most pressing
concern to planning formative evaluation is the
specificity of the evaluation focus.

Specificity of Focus. When programs are
discussed holistically by candidates or by
graduates, there is less possibility that
implications drawn from such comments will be
implemented. For example, if candidates report
that the teacher education program should give
more attention to matters of classroom
discipline, teacher education faculty may find
the suggestion of interest, but each individual
faculty member might regard the advice as
something to be acted upon in someone else's
class. To overcome this problem, formative
evaluation can solicit findings in the form of
comments, suggestions or problems, and
strengths in connection with specific courses.
Recommendations about Education 101, rather
than about the teacher education program in
general, are likely to get more serious
attention.

A concern not listed in the formulations
of Katz, et al. (1981) includes the following:

Relevance of Focus to Program Design. The
thrust of a formative evaluation should be to
inquire if the program is implemented as
designed. Of course, if there is no design, or
if the design is only implicit, it will be
difficult to carry out an effective formative
evaluation. If that is the case, the work
should turn to the creation of the needed
program design. However, if programs do indeed
meet the NCATE Standard I.A relating to the
Design of the Curriculum, then there is a firm
basis for planning an effective formative
evaluation. So often, formative evaluations
collect data not related to curriculum design

issues. For example, questionnaires used as instruments to elicit data from candidates about program implementation may ask for valuative comments about how much they "liked" or "disliked" a particular program or program element. In formative evaluation, the question might better be put, "Was a particular element in place?" Whether the candidates "liked" it or not is of secondary importance in a formative evaluation.

A third issue needs to be reviewed when planning a formative evaluation. Fox (1982) advocates a concern for engaging those to be evaluated in the process of planning an evaluation design.

Responsiveness of Focus. Fox (1982) suggests that those designing the evaluation program and those implementing it should be involved in the intellectual demands associated with planning the formative evaluation and interpreting the results. Program designers and implementors need to tackle some of the substantive and methodological problems in applying the formative evaluation. Evaluation, according to Fox, is not an activity that is left to technicians to conduct, interpret, and report.

These issues, then, may represent some of the "missing links" in formative evaluation that in the past have rendered the enterprise, at least, impotent, if not problematic. When designing a formative evaluation for the University of Florida teacher education program, these elements need to be examined.

PLANNING THE EVALUATION

Assume for the moment that we are charged with the responsibility of organizing, planning, and carrying out the evaluation. This charge may have come from the chair of the department that offers the program at the University of Florida, from that department's Executive Committee, or from its Curriculum Committee. Assume also that we have received a legitimate directive to carry out the evaluation. Assume, further, that we have collected as much information about the program's design as summarized in the opening pages of this paper. The next step in the process is to engage the faculty in planning the formative evaluation.

Engaging the Faculty. We will design the formative evaluation by collaborating with the faculty who designed and implemented the program. The issue here is whether or not the program was implemented as planned. The faculty is probably concerned about different elements of the program design. For example, there may be more doubt about the ways in which seminars are conducted than about how the methods instruction is delivered. There may be more concern about how well cooperating teachers are supporting the goals in the field experience than in the implementation of the role playing exercises. Nevertheless, we need to engage the faculty in identifying those problematic elements and to focus the evaluation on those elements.

The evaluation could also focus on some positive elements, items the faculty deem to be in good shape. In addition, the design could allow for candidates, cooperating teachers, and instructors to include openended comments in their responses. These may direct subsequent inquiry into what had been considered non-problematic areas. The faculty will not only be engaged in helping narrow the focus of the evaluation; they will also contribute to the interpretation of the findings.

Anyone who has worked with program faculty, in the public schools or in higher education, understands the difficulty of helping colleagues arrive at some sort of consensus about program goals. It is important to find an agreement that accommodates the positions of individuals participating in the process but not to the extent of jeopardizing the group consensus.

One promising approach to use is the "paired comparison" method (see Figure 1). In

Directions: Those elements of our program
nominated as a concern are paired with one
another below.   In each pairing, circle the
element that is of greater concern to you.

Elements: A: seminar
           B: substantive panel (foundations)
           C: substantive panel (methods)
           D: field experiences

Pairings: (Circle only one in each pair)

           1. A vs B
           2. A vs C
           3. A vs D
           4. B vs C
           5. B vs D
           6. C vs D

Figure 1.   Paired Comparisons: Program Elements
of Concern.

applying   this   procedure,   the   faculty   and
perhaps other stakeholders,   such as the   dean,
candidates   and   representatives of the   public
school,   might   share   thoughts   about   which
elements of the program are most problematic
or about which of the elements of our program
are   not   being implemented with   the   fidelity
promised in the program design.   The discussion
sets   the   dimension on which a   comparison   is
wanted.   It   may involve some disagreements   on
areas or on priorities. Those elements that are
advanced or nominated as a faculty concern   are
entered   into   a   rating   form   such   as   the
following   taken   from our   University   Florida
example.
      Assume   that   there   are   twenty   program
faculty participating in this exercise.   There
would   be   120   total   votes registered   on   the
forms.   The maximum number of times any element
could   be   cited by a faculty member   would   be
three, so the highest possible score an element
could receive is sixty.

If the distribution were perfectly flat, with A, B, C, and D getting approximately equal numbers of citations, nothing would have been gained from this exercise, except perhaps to learn that all four elements are viewed equally as problematic by the faculty as a group; thus, all four should be included in the evaluation focus. But assume, on the other hand, that very few faculty circled B, the substantive panel focused on foundation. This result may suggest that it is the consensus of the faculty that this element could be omitted from this round of formative evaluation.

This procedure could also be used to inquire about more concrete program elements needing study within each of the components. If, indeed, there is a concern about the methods component, we could then find and describe the dimension of comparison on which data are desired. Then we would nominate elements of that component and ask faculty to carry out a paired comparison activity to discover whether a consensus exists concerning those particular elements in the evaluation design.

Relevance of the Evaluation. We need to collect data that are relevant to the program design and, more specifically, to the narrowed focus that may have resulted from the first step of our planning. One approach here is to have the faculty conduct "thought experiments" about hypothetical data. In planning an hypothetical evaluation, Popham (1981) recommends preparing a mock report containing fictitious data and then in the content, structure, or style of the report, ask if there were omissions, deletions, or redunancies. Such a mock evaluation report can prove heuristically helpful in such settings." (p. 7). Our point in adopting the Popham suggestion would be to assure that the data were relevant to our evaluation goals. To augment the Popham suggestion, we should consider the following hypothetical data concerning the University of Florida program. Candidates in the program are asked, hypothetically, to respond to the following questions on a five-point Likert scale, ranging from 1 (this element not observed) to 5 (this element almost always present). The two elements under study include: (A) instructors are punitive when candidates make error in their teaching, and (B) teaching methods in the program are congruent with the goals of the program. Imagine the faculty's response if the mean of Item A were 4.2 with a standard deviation of 0.15, and what if the mean of Item B were 2.3 with a standard deviation of 1.6? If the faculty cannot think of a specific improvement, change, or intervention when confronted with these examples, or if they cannot imagine some other configuration of the findings, then the sources yielding the real data represented in this exercise would not be tapped.

Strategies of Data Collection. Ideally, a thorough evaluation of a teacher education program would use a cadre of trained observers; however, the cost is likely to be prohibitive. Further, this approach can be highly reactive. Observers can change what is occurring in the classroom or in the laboratory for the period of time they are present. Whether or not what they see is representative of what goes on daily in the classroom daily becomes arguable. Steele, House, and Kerins (1971) proposed a solution to this problem that is feasible for formative evaluation efforts in teacher education. Instead of asking pupils, in a program for the gifted, whether or not they liked the program or thought the program was effective, the instrument elicited from pupils a decription of what was happening in the classroom. In effect, this approach engaged pupils as "informants". For our purposes, as it was for those of Steele et al., it is an interesting solution. Candidates are in the classroom most of the time, unlike a paid observer who would occasionally drop in. Since candidates are part of the scenery, asking them to report on the program elements implemented diminishes the reactivity caused by paid observers. Finally, if the questions are sufficiently clear, then the candidates can respond to them with confidence. In such an effort, not only would average group responses be of interest but, also, the associated standard deviations. For instance, if there was agreement within a class that the instructor did assign book reports, we might assume with some confidence that, indeed, the instructor did assign book reports. On the other hand, if there was disagreement here, indicated by the standard deviation of the responses, we might attribute less confidence to the findings.

This description is not to suggest that this approach is without problems. At one time, we asked our candidates at the University of Illinois to estimate how many times they were supervised. We also asked our supervisors to give us a record of how many times they had supervised each of their student teachers. As you might guess, the two means were not close in value. The supervisors reported they supervised the candidates more frequently than the student teachers said they were supervised. On further study, we discovered that student teachers did not count a visit as a "supervisory" occasion unless there was a face to face interview after the observation. Such bizarre interpretations cannot be prevented, and the data collected from such efforts need to be studied warily.

Note that the candidates in the Steele et al. effort were not being asked to rate how well they liked the elements of the program. Candidates were asked to report if the elements relevant to the program design were stressed in the course. It is not the case, then, that candidates are evaluating the program. Instead, they are providing the evaluators with data which describe the implementation of the program. In a similar manner, we could engage our candidates in the process of describing the program delivered to them.

More specifically, the instrument to be
used in our formative evaluation of the Florida
program, assuming that it elicits data the
faculty would find relevant and informative,
might look something like this:

Section I: (Demographic Information)

Section II: Base your answer on how well   each
sentence describes what is stressed in   your
class--what the instructor in this class does
or asks you to do.   Darken only one answer per
sentence.
(Assume that under every sentence there are
four   "bubbles" labeled strongly agree, agree,
disagree, strongly disagree.)

1.   The   instructor   taught this   course   in   a
     manner similar to how he/she would like you
     to teach.
2.   The   instructor   encourages candidates   to
     examine   their   mistakes and   formulate
     possible corrections.
3.   The   instructor   encourages candidates   to
     discover   "personal   meaning"   in   the
     information that is shared in class.
4.   The   instruction in this course is based on
     a few important concepts rather   than   on
     many "facts" about teaching.
5.   (Other similar items based on the   premises
     of the program design).

Section III: Share here any concerns you have
about this course or the teacher education
program in general.

                 (Space provided)

Figure 2.   Teacher Education Program
Questionnaire.

A variation on this approach can inquire about the degree to which certain topics have been covered in a program component. For example, in the program at the University of Florida, the methods course is offered via activity packages which are intended to cover the elements usually included in the course. Specific questions concerning coverage can be administered with an instrument similar to that sketched above. For example,

---

Section I: Demographics

Section II: Base your answer on how well each sentence describes what was stressed in the activities you undertook in that component of our program assigned to the "Substantive Panel". Darken only one answer per sentence. (Assume that under each sentence there are four bubbles, marked strongly agree, agree, disagree and strongly disagree).

1. Reciprocal teaching was stressed in this component of the program.
2. Mastery teaching was stressed in this component of the program.
3. Cooperative learning was stressed in this component of the program.
4. The framing of the U.S. Constitution was stressed in this component of the program.
5. (Others reflecting the elements which the design assigned to the Substantive Panel component and perhaps others, such as Number 4 above, which were not.

Section III: Share any concerns you have with the Substantive Panel component, or any other concerns you have about the program.

(Space provided)

Figure 3. Substantive Panel Questionnaire.

A third variation on the Steele et al. procedure seeks to assess how confident candidates are in the degree to which they have learned specific content. Instead of merely asking if the content was stressed in class, the items in this questionnaire ask about the extent to which the content has been learned. Groteluschen and Harnisch at the University of Illinois have used such a scale, based in part on Broudy's notions of "proficiency" to assess the knowledge of professionals in an accountancy program. While they have not yet published their results, they have been impressed with the promise of this technique. They have observed that those rating the items high are candidates nominated by instructors as top performers in the class. Such an instrument, adapted for teacher education, is shown in Figure 4 (next page).

It is assumed that those elements in the content area that receive high ratings across the row are those that the candidates have mastered. When there is a high rating in the left hand column and lower ratings in the right hand columns, it may suggest that topics are covered but not taught. If low marks exist at all levels, perhaps the topics are not even covered in the course. As before, bogus elements could be introduced into the column at the left to get a measure of how seriously candidates are taking the exercise. If one of the elements on the left were "operant conditioning", and this was not one of the topics in the program, we would expect it to receive low ratings from most of our candidates, excepting those perhaps who have had instruction in or an abiding interest in Skinner's work.

CAVEATS

Of course the psychometric properties of the scales and instruments advanced here for the use in a teacher education formative evaluation program need to be investigated. While these

Directions: As a professional educator, the knowledge you possess is used in different ways. For each "use" of knowledge found in the column headings to the right, rate your ability to perform in that mode concerning each teacher education content area found in the left hand column. Enter a number from 1 (can't perform at all) to 10 (Can perform extremely well) in each of the blanks.

Content Area	Converse about the content in general ways.	Give explanations about elements of the content.	Coach others in the use of the content.
Reciprocal teaching			
Cooperative learning			
Other elements of content to be covered by the course or program component			

Figure 4. Teacher Education Knowledge Proficiency Scale.

scales and these approaches may be used successfully elsewhere, the key question is, "How reliable are the ratings emanating from their use at the University of Florida?"

Second, Robert Stake admonishes us not to advocate procedures that have not been used successfully at some site. While pieces of the elements in the design proposed here have been used in evaluation efforts, I am unaware of any program in which this sort of design has been implemented.

Third, nothing here has addressed the question about whether or not the University of Florida program is right in doing what it is doing. That is, summative evaluation has been ignored.

SUMMARY

This paper has addressed ways of undertaking a formative evaluation of a teacher education program. It has grounded its suggestions in a concern that the evaluation effort be responsive to the information needs of the persons planning and delivering the program and also to the need for specific information about distinctive elements of the program--its assumptions and premises. A hypothetical program was described, and the elements of the program were built into the proposed instruments to be used in the evaluation. The paper closed with several cautions about the suggestions included herein.

REFERENCES

Brandt, R. S. (Ed.). (1981). **Applied Strategies for Curriculum Evaluation.** Alexandria, VA: Association for Supervision and Curriculum Development.

Combs, A. W. (1965). **The professional education of teachers.** Boston: Allyn and Bacon. (Note: The description ofthe hypothetical program was taken in part from Atkin, J. M. and Raths, J. D., "Changing Patterns of Teacher Education in the United States", a report prepared for the Directorate for Scientific Affairs, Organization for Economic Cooperation and Development, 1974).

Fox, Jr. G. T. (1982). Can a federal program
be field responsive, policy relevant and
professionally illuminative? Paper
presented to the 1981 Annual Meeting of
the American Educational Research
Association, Los Angeles.

Katz, L., et al. (1981). Follow-up Studies:
Are they worth the trouble? **Journal of
Teacher Education**, 32(2), 18-23.

National Council for the Accreditation of
Teacher Education. (1986). **NCATE
Standards, Procedures and Policies for the
Accreditation of Professional Teacher
Education Units.** Washington: NCATE.

Nelli, E. and Nutter, N. (1984). **A Model for
Evaluating Teacher Education Programs.**
Washington: American Assoication of
Colleges for Teacher Education. (ERIC
Document Reproduction Service No. 251 406)

Popham, W. J. (1981). The Evaluator's
curse. In R. S. Brandt, (Ed.) **Applied
Strategies for Curriculum Evaluation.**
Alexandria, VA: Association for
Supervision and Curriculum Development.

Steele, J. M., House, E. R. & Kerins, T.
(1971). An instrument for assessing
instructional climate through low-
inference student judgements. **American
Educational Research Journal.** 8, 447-466.

ABOUT THE AUTHOR

James D. Raths, Dean of the College of
Education and Social Services and Professor of
Education at the University of Vermont, was
formerly at the University of Illinois, the
University of Maryland, and the University of
Wisconsin-Milwaukee. He received the Ph.D. in
Research and Evaluation from New York
University in 1960. Since then he has served
as a consultant to a variety of public and
private agencies on program evaluation. He is
the author of over seventy-five articles on
various aspects of teacher education and has
served as Consulting Editor or Executive Editor
of **The Science Teacher** and the **Journal of
Educational Research.** His current research
interest is in the improvement of teacher
education programs through evaluation.

3

THE PROFESSIONAL EDUCATION UNIT

Richard C. Kunkel
National Council For Accreditation
of Teacher Education

A "professional education unit" is the body responsible for the preparation of teachers and other professional education personnel. A "unit" generally consists of administrative, policy, program (selected courses and field experiences), and staff components. A "professional education unit" has the ultimate responsibility for planning and operating a professional teacher education program. It may be a school, college, department or other administrative body within that institution. In discussions of professionalism in education and in accreditation the "professional education unit" is usually referred to as "the unit."

The unit was one of the six elements focused on in the May 1987 conference on "Teacher Education Evaluation: Some Missing Links." In preparing for this presentation five items surfaced along with a statement that was meant to be casual encouragement. Those items were:

1. The unit as a professional focus: Theory and practice,
2. The impact of unit focus on other related agencies,
3. Tenets of quality unit evaluation.
4. Accreditation as one form of unit evaluation, and
5. Developing practices related to program in the education unit.

These tasks won't be easy. However, it is becoming imperative that institutions seek every avenue to improve programs for the preparation of teachers. The five items above are keys to success in carrying out a quality program.

THE UNIT AS A PROFESSIONAL FOCUS: THEORY AND DEVELOPMENT

As America grows and matures, systems become more and more specialized. Specialization leads, among other things, to calls for field definition. What are the boundaries of a profession? Who has the right/responsibility to answer those questions? Who should say that **X** is/is not a profession? How is the jurisdiction question answered? Intermingled with these items are concerns about preparation of the next cadre of professionals. How should their preparation to practice in the profession be conducted? And under whose auspices? These questions and many others must be resolved.

In many fields, professional training and definition of the field are tied closely together. That is not the case in professional education. The preparation of school-based personnel is not as directly tied to the definition of the field. During the past fifteen years the Council on Postsecondary Accreditation (COPA) has played a dominant role over the profession.

COPA's publication, **The Balance Wheel for Accreditation** (July 1986) provides a definition of the major areas of professionalism in our

society.   COPA recognizes accreditation as the
link   between   program   preparation   for
professionals and the arena of practice.

COPA   deals   with   institutions   and   other
agencies.   The   focus   is   preparation   for
practice   (both   at   entry   level   and   advanced
practice).   About seventy-five specialty areas
and   eight   institutional accrediting   agencies
are recognized by the agency.

When   an   education agency uses   the   COPA
definition   as its mission, that   agency   will
find   that   the   National   Council   for
Accreditation   of Teacher Education (NCATE)   is
recognized   as the body to "define   the   field"
for   the preparation of teachers.   The   U.   S.
Department   of Education is also a   participant
in   "defining   the field."   This parallels   the
definition of the professional as found in law,
medicine,   social   work,   business   and   other
professions.   Again,   because   of   COPA
definitions, that jurisdiction covers education
from   preschool   through   grade   12.   The
conceptual definition of the field therefore is
established.   It   involves   those   areas   of
preparation for service as professional school-
based   personnel.   This   includes   the   entire
range   of studies (e.g.,   teachers of English,
social   studies,   mathematics   and   for   the
elementary   grades).   It   also   encompasses
counselors, administrators, and other positions
for   which   individuals   are   traditionally
licensed   by states   to function in   and   with
schools.   This constitutes "the unit."

THE IMPACT OF UNIT FOCUS ON OTHER RELATED AGENCIES

In   January 1983 a report was presented to   the
American   Association of Colleges   for   Teacher
Education.   The   title   of that report   was   **A
Proposed   Accreditation system (an   alternative
to   the   current NCATE system).**   The   report's
major proposition was future accreditation of a
professional   unit   should   be   based   on   the
continuing   evaluation   of   that   professional

education unit. That point was made clearly and continuously by Scannell, et al., (January 1983). The NCATE redesign that became effective in 1986 called for evaluation throughout the accreditation process and procedure.

The redesign is clear about the unit's mission. The mission is stated in five categories of standards. Nineteen standards are distributed through those five categories, and there are 94 criteria for demonstrating that a unit is in compliance with the accreditation standards. A unit seeking accreditation must meet eleven preconditions to start the accreditation process. The structure of the redesign states that a unit seeking accreditation must demonstrate its ability to meet rigorous national standards for the preparation and support of high quality programs for the preparation of teachers and school personnel.

There is a logic to the five categories of standards and to the order of their presentation. The five categories are:

Category I   Knowledge Base for Professional
               Education
Category II   Relationship to the World of
               Practice
Category III   Students
Category IV   Faculty
Category V   Governance and Resources

The primary reason for being is the development, maintenance, and distribution of a body of professional knowledge (Category I) that should be known by a professional teacher. In order to use the knowledge base two ideas must be kept in mind: (1) The knowledge base is large, incomplete, and interpretable in many ways. Professionals in the field should use the knowledge base to expand it. (2) The knowledge base should be used to help learners from preschool to grade 12 accomplish their growth objectives.

To learn how to foster and nurture learning in the elementary through secondary grades, an organized set of field experiences is needed. Those activities require that the relationship to the world of work be established (Category II). Building that relationship is important in the on-going work of the teacher.

The third category of standards pertains to the individuals preparing to be teachers. The development and use of a body of professional knowledge and establishing a sequence of field experiences would be without reason if a cadre of students were not there to be served. There are two groups to be served, the elementary and secondary students. Their growth goals for the students are:

1. Academic growth;
2. Physical, socio, and emotional growth;
3. Growth in the language arts (i.e., reading, writing, speaking, and listening);
4. Growth in mathematical problem solving;
5. Learning how to learn; and
6. Growth of productive citizenry.

One of the reasons that education is such a difficult arena is the fact that there is a second set of learners involved; the teacher candidates. These people have a different set of educational goals. These include:

1. Earning a major in an area of specialty offered at the educational unit. (i.e., a major in physics, chemistry, literature, home economics, and elementary education);
2. Earning credit for the composite of courses that defines the elements of a liberal or general education;
3. Satisfactorily completing courses on the didactics of education including instructional and learning theories, history, sociological and psychological foundations of education, principles of instruction, methods of instruction, and educational practices and techniques; and

4. Satisfactorily completing a set of field
    experiences including observation of
    teaching, serving as a teacher's assistant,
    tutor, and student teaching.

These two sets of objectives are in essence
BOTH ULTIMATE OUTCOMES. High positive
accomplishment on either one of them does not
guarantee the other (Category III). Our
mission is clear. It is to accomplish BOTH
goals: to satisfy the requirements to become a
teacher; and, to help our pupils learn how to
learn.
        The fourth factor is faculty. There are
many areas in which teachers are unnecessary.
The accrediting process assumes the need for
faculty that can and will guide the learning of
the teacher education candidates. NCATE has
listed as compliance criteria the types,
numbers, and degree requirements needed for
accreditation (Category IV).
        The last dimension or category deals with
the unit's governance and resources (Category
V). A central premise of the accreditation
process is the fact the unit cannot function
without governance. Rules and regulations are
needed to maintain uniformity in the product
of the accreditation process. And finally,
without resources (i.e., physical, material,
informational, and human resources) the system
experiences difficulty. High quality teacher
education has a large price tag. To be
certified as a producer of high quality
teachers requires their identification and
recruitment.
        Prior to 1987 the accrediting process
focused on programs for various teaching
specialties (such as history, mathematics,
school counselors, etc). A self-study and a
site visit were conducted. The purpose of
self-study was to determine if sufficient
criteria for compliance were documented. The
purpose of the site visit was, in part, a
validity check of the self-study. The site
visit team examined the evidence needed to
substantiate the self study. If enough

evidence was verified, the program was granted accreditation. If too little evidence or inappropriate evidence was found the petition for accreditation on a particular specialty was denied. If all the other specialties more than met the criteria of compliance, the transcripts of students in the successful departments would have NCATE approved stamped on them indicating they had completed an approved program. The transcripts of the students in the one program that failed to establish compliance would not receive an approval stamp.

The redesign which went into effect in 1986 changed the process and the criteria. In the words of the redesign, a change was made to a "unit" focus. The self-study and the on-site visit components were retained. The change was made for those instances in which a UNIT offered two or more professional programs. If each of those programs presented enough evidence to document compliance to the standards, a UNIT was awarded full accreditation. If one (or more) of the areas of program specialty failed to establish compliance to the standards, that UNIT's total program may be denied accreditation or accredited with stipulations.

Clearly, NCATE's policies, practices, and procedures are built on the assumption that the educational unit is the center for educational evaluation. Through this unit focus, NCATE concentrates on the demonstrated ability of the professional education unit to meet rigorous national standards for the preparation and support of high quality preparation of teachers and school personnel.

What does this mean to higher education and state agencies? The effect on higher education follows precedents established by other professions. NCATE is governed by the education profession, both the practicing and training arms and others who have a stake in the outcomes of professional education programs. In other professions the educational accountability and responsibility is targeted to programs within a unit. This targeted responsibility guides both national accreditation and many state accreditation programs.

The unit focus gives the profession some leverage in its efforts to improve programs for the preparation of teachers. Consider the instance of a professional education unit that offers five program specialties--one of which is a considerable distance from being in compliance with the NCATE Standards. In the past that program could continue to offer preparation in the area of specialty with little pressure to change. The redesign enlists the other four programs in effecting change. Pressure on the offending program may expedite improvement.

The move to a unit focus has the potential to impact higher education in a variety of ways. First the unit focus may provoke action aimed at the offending program and aid in bringing it up to standard. This is the probable impact when "accredited with stipulation." In this case, a bill of particulars is presented to the unit stating the needed items for achieving compliance. A second form of impact is the excising of programs that probably should have been terminated earlier.

The move to the unit focus strengthens NCATE's control over the profession and, in so doing, gains greater control of the evaluation of teacher education. The redesign makes the unit the substance by which an evaluation paradigm can be structured. NCATE can base teacher education evaluation on the formative-summative approach to evaluation (Scriven, 1967). It can form an NCATE evaluation along the systematic (context, input, process and product evaluation), approach of Stufflebeam, et al. (1971), or on the holistic approach of Stake (1967).

The unit becomes the substance by which an evaluation paradigm can be designed. It allows both the "knowledge base of program evaluation" and the "knowledge base of the unit" to serve as the substance of program evaluation.

Another impact of the "unit" focus is the
elimination of what Schulman (1987) referred to
as a "pedestrian view" rather than "the
professional view." That means that teacher
education candidates would receive preparation
that is different than that received by all
college students in a liberal arts or a general
studies program.

The impact of the "unit" focus on state
agencies is on the regulating and the
academic/collegial functions. State agencies
identify more with the role of the regulatory,
that is, the authorizing of licenses. The unit
approach allows the state to use the
accreditation process in the same ways it is
used by states in addressing professional
development in other fields. In recent years
much redundancy has developed. The overlap is
on the state's role in regulating and the
profession's role of certification and
accreditation. The Carnegie Forum's proposal
(1986) has brought more light to this topic.
The unit focus in building the profession has
been the focus of publications by the American
Federation of Teachers and the National
Education Association and in **Education Week**
(1987, April). These jurisdictional problems
need further discussion.

Evaluation of the professional unit must
be based on the validity of the training. This
is contrary to the perception that only outcome
measurement is necessary. The "unit" focus is
a statement about the need for program
continuity in the preparation of professional
educators. Most evaluators, researchers, and
thoughtful citizens know that restricting
evaluation to a single measure is far too
limited.

TENETS OF QUALITY UNIT EVALUATION

Quality evaluation of professional education
units requires attention to three items.
Effective evaluation of a unit must be

holistic, deal with hard and soft data, and be continually future oriented.

A holistic approach addresses the many dimensions of the entity being evaluated in an integrated manner. This is reflected in the merger of the 19 standards, the 94 criteria of compliance, the eleven preconditions, and the annual reports into a total package for initial and continuing accreditation. A holistic evaluation of the quality of an educational unit attempts to encompass multiple standards from various points of view. Certainly, there will be instances in which a unit will design and conduct studies of interest to the individuals in the particular unit. Such studies should be encouraged and facilitated.

The evaluation to be undertaken should not be restricted to "number crunching." Teacher education evaluation encompasses much from the affective domain. Too many people place connotations of "goodness" and "badness" on data. To those people, we do not "know" if we cannot count and measure some entity. Others contend that we fail to find and use "real data" until and unless we submerge ourselves in the item being studied. The differences on the part of the people who enjoin this debate ought to put it to rest. The principle that is sought is clear. We cannot reject ANY form of data OUT-OF-HAND. Different epistemologies require differing kinds of data interpreted in differing ways.

Program evaluation needs to be future oriented and continuous. This is reflected not only in the NCATE Standards, but also by the requirement of an on-going systematic evaluation of our graduates as they become professionals in the field.

Recent leaders in engineering admonish teacher education to plan for change and improvement. Improvement doesn't just happen; it is planned and planned for.

Accreditation as a Form of Evaluation

Accreditation is a form of evaluation. In particular it is evaluation in which the item(s) being evaluated are instructional programs. Accreditation is a problem focused process: the problem is structured by the question, "Which, for my purposes, is the best professional education unit?" In both accreditation and program evaluation we deal with values and valuating. Both evaluation and accreditation are situation specific. They both focus on the same programs, the same dimensions of value, the same clients. Their differences are in the breadth of concern. Evaluation is the broader term, accreditation is more prescribed. They are sufficiently alike to accept the argument: evaluation and accreditation are both forms of solving of complex problems; and problematic because they deal with decisions about the value and worth of the program options.

Accreditation as One Form of Unit Evaluation

The tenets of quality accreditation leads to the conclusion that an efficient, effective, quality-oriented approach to accreditation can serve as an evaluation of the professional education unit. Accreditation serves in many educational specialties. A review indicated that 21 professional organizations ranging from those responsible for early childhood education, to state superintendents, and state boards of education made up NCATE (Gollnick & Kunkel, 1986).

The following assumptions are related to both accreditation and evaluation.

1. The value of systematically aggregated data is an intergral part of both problem solving processes.
2. The internal self-study and internal needs assessment are important components of the accreditation process. They involve staff

directly, a principle vital in effecting change and improvement.
3. The external review and qualitative judgement assures quality data and its interpretation. These are important aspects of both processes.

Developing Practices Related to Program Evaluation in the Professional Education Unit

In the preparation of teachers and other school based personnel, the place of program evaluation is significant and critical. It is infused in the redesign standards, policies and procedures of NCATE. Evaluation is first noted as a precondition in the NCATE standards document (page 8, number 4) which requires that

>   the unit keeps abreast of emerging evaluation techniques and regularly monitors and evaluates, both internally and externally, its operation, scope, quality of its offerings, and effectiveness of its graduates.

This adaptation of the previous standard (6.1) is now a precondition and must be clearly established with evidence prior to the continued accreditation of a professional education unit. This precondition calls for an understanding of the field of program evaluation and developments in that field.
Studies have been conducted systematically over the last 15 years to keep abreast of developments in the area of program evaluation. (Hebel, unpublished). Practices for developing evaluation of program can also be found in Category II Relationship to the World of Practice (Standard II.B, compliance criteria 1 and 2). Those points read as follows:

>   (1) The unit keeps abreast of emerging evaluation techniques and

engages in regular and systematic evaluation to determine the success and quality of graduates in the professional education roles for which they were prepared, and (2) Follow-up studies of graduates are used by the unit to assess the relevance of professional education objectives and to modify and improve the program(s) appropriately. (p. 32).

Continued use of program evaluation, practices, techniques and findings are an important and an integral part of the redesign of the NCATE Standards of the accreditation of programs for the approval of teacher education programs.

TASK THAT WON'T BE EASY

The points presented in the five areas of discussion above depict a topic of much importance and relevance. It is clear that several limiting circumstances exist that will not be easy to overcome. They include:

1. Focus on a professional unit as a whole is contrary to the way individual faculty members function (and many times their departments). Typically faculty find their pride, esteem, and collegiality by identifying with their particular program. (i.e., school administration, counseling, and special education). Seldom is the concern with the total unit.
2. Too often professional walls have been built around departments and programs. The development of knowledge bases and expertise has suffered because of limits of the audience involved. Other exceptions exist. The American Educational Research Association, the Association of Teacher Educators, and other national organizations have brought attention to the

interrelationships of the whole unit. This is generally not the way professionals see, set, and maintain their jurisdictional lines.
3. Because regulation and state licensure is tied directly to functional roles, the profession is divided along the lines of certification and licensure. A clear understanding of the relationship between regulation, and the building of a profession through certification and accreditation should and would clarify these issues.

In closing, the professional unit is an important element for the preparation of teachers and school personnel and must serve as a point of discussion for program evaluation and accreditation. This view must be supported, developed and encouraged throughout the profession.

REFERENCES

Carnegie Task Force on Teaching as a Profession. (1986). **A nation prepared: teachers for the twenty-first centruy.** New York: Carnegie Forum on Education and the Economy.
Council on Postsecondary Accreditation. (1986). **The balance wheel for accreditation.** Washington: COPA.
Gollnick, D. M., & Kunkel, R. C. (1986, December). The reform of national accreditation. **Phi Delta Kappan, 68,** 310-314.
Hebel, T. (1985 July). **A comparison of the evaluation practices of NCATE accredited teacher education institutions and the context, input, process and product evaluation model.** Unpublished doctoral dissertation proposal, Northern Illinois University, DeKalb, IL.

National Council for the Accreditation of Teacher Education. (1986, October). **Standards, Procedures, Policies for the Accreditation of Professional Teacher Education Units.** Washington: NCATE.

Rodman, B. (1987, April 1). N.E.A. pursues its plan to establish state boards controlled by teachers. **Education Week,** 6(31), 1.

Scannell, D. P., Gardner, W. E., Olsen, H. C., Sullivan, C. & Wisniewski, R. (1983 January). **A proposed accreditation system (An alternative to the current NCATE System).** Washington: American Association of Colleges for Teacher Education.

Schulman, L. (1987, February). **Ensuring teacher quality.** Paper presented at the meeting of the American Association of Colleges for Teacher Education.

Scriven, M. (1967). The methodology of evaluation. In Smith, B. O. (ed.). **Perspectives of Curriculum Evaluation.** (AERA Monograph Series on Curriculum Evaluation). Chicago: Rand McNally.

Stake, R. E. (1967). The countenance of educational evaluation. **Teachers College Record** 68(7), 523-540.

Stufflebeam, D. L. (1968). Toward a science of educational evaluation **Educational Technology.** 8, 5-12.

Stufflebeam, D. L., Foley, W. J., Gephart, W. J., Guba, E. G., Hammond, R. L., Merriam, H. O., & Provus, M. M. (1971). **Educational evaluation and decision-making.** Bloomington, IN: Phi Delta Kappa National Study Committee.

ABOUT THE AUTHOR

Richard C. Kunkel, Executive Director of the National Council for Accreditation of Teacher Education, formerly served as Dean of the College of Education at the University of Nevada at Las Vegas, Chair of the Department of Education at St. Louis University, and Instructor at Ball State University and in the Burris Laboratory School at that institution. He received the Ph.D. from St. Louis University with major emphasis in administration and curriculum. He has published widely and served as a consultant to such organizations and projects as AID programs, to Teacher Corps and teacher centers, the Lilly Endowment and Danforth Foundation, and as a long term evaluator to Cities in Schools and various bilingual and Hispanic education projects.

4

AN OUTCOMES-BASED TEACHER PREPARATION PROGRAM

Donald M. Medley
University of Virginia

INTRODUCTION

As members of higher education faculties, society sees us as being in the knowledge business. The role of higher education is to develop research based knowledge and transmit it to students. Many of our critics across the campus, the state, and the country deny that teacher educators perform either role. They deny that there is any research based knowledge relevant to the practice of teaching. They assert instead that professors of education function as master teachers who pass on the accumulated folklore of teaching to apprentices--a function schools can do better than the institution of higher education can.

These beliefs are shared by the public, by its legislative representatives, by any of our own graduates and by many of us. If they are true, then higher education has no legitimate role in the professional preparation of teachers and our programs deserve to die. I strongly disagree with both of these points. I believe that the role of college and university based teacher education programs is critically important; that without a firm base in research and theory the practice of teaching will continue to fail to provide the majority of American children with the education they need. But unless we can convince those who have the power to destroy us that these beliefs are sound, destroy us is exactly what they will do. The only question is, when?

At this point no convincing evidence exists that a body of relevant research based knowledge exists or that teacher education programs transmit such knowledge to the graduating students who are recommended as competent teachers. There is no evidence that our students know how to teach any better or are any more effectively than teachers who lack such preparation. I will not belabor this point any longer; I have brought it up only to underscore how important it is that this conference lead to action. If we can document the outcomes our programs produce, if we can confirm that students who complete our programs do acquire functional knowledge about teaching and learning not elsewhere available, we will go a long way toward solving the problem of evaluating the outcomes of teacher education.

To document the results of teacher education, the central focus of a teacher preparation program must be the assessment of that program's outcomes. We have the capability to assess these outcomes well enough, often enough and easily enough to convince our students, ourselves and those who would destroy us of the importance of what we do. We must readily and thoroughly exploit what we already know about the evaluation of teaching. To illustrate this point, I will sketch the design for an **Outcomes-Based Teacher Preparation Program.**

AN OUTCOMES-BASED TEACHER PREPARATION PROGRAM

The outcomes-based teacher preparation program prepares students who have never taught for

certification as competent to teach. The
status of each student is known at every stage
of progress through the program, and the
program is continuously focused on program
outcomes.

The first event that an entering student
would experience is an exercise designed to
measure and assess that student's status with
respect to program outcomes. Assessment would
be repeated regularly until achievement of
those outcomes was evidenced. At that point,
the student would graduate from the program and
be recommended for certification.

Each assessment exercise would consist of
a series of typical teaching problems arranged
to simulate a normal day of teaching. The
problems would be presented in a variety of
modes; some in the form of videotapes of
classroom behavior, others in the form of brief
verbal vignettes. In most cases, the student
would respond by marking one of several
alternative answers or solutions to each
problem on an Opscan sheet, much like those
used for ordinary paper and pencil
examinations.

Each assessment exercise would be
equivalent in difficulty to every other
exercise. All students would be required to
deal with the same problems regardless of how
long they had been enrolled or what courses
they had taken. Compared to conventional
programs, the students' first experiences
would give them a much more accurate idea of
what these outcomes are, a sense of what
teaching is like. Subsequent experiences would
indicate how much progress they were making.
The principal function of the exercises would
be to ascertain and document the degree to
which each student had achieved program
outcomes at each stage in theprogress through
it.

These exercises would differ sharply from
typical college examinations. None would be
identified with any course or subject, so that
the student would have no clues to the
knowledge or skills needed to do well. No

single exercise would be recognizable as an examination in psychology, methods of teaching, philosophy of education, or specific area. Each one would be a test of the students' ability to deal with typical teaching problems. The problems a teacher encounters on the job are not determined by which courses the teacher may have had, nor are they determined by problems a student encounters in one of these assessment exercises. This is surely one reason why paper and pencil tests, although fair measures of the abilities students need to succeed in college, are very poor measures of the abilities they need to succeed as teachers. The assessment exercises used in the outcomes-based teacher preparation program are designed to address abilities of the latter type and to be insensitive to abilities of the former type.

Since the only knowledge that a teacher can use to solve problems encountered while teaching is knowledge she can access at that point in time, the ability to access knowledge on demand is vitally important. Conventional examinations do not measure this ability; that is why teachers' scores on even the best paper and pencil tests, such as the National Teacher Examination, do not correlate with teacher performance or teacher effectiveness.

Teaching differs from test taking in another important way. Course examinations include only questions whose answers have been taught; therefore, every problem on a test has at least one right answer. But life is less considerate. Not all of the problems a teacher encounters have a right answer. Some problems may have more than one acceptable solution but no ideal one. Others may have no acceptable solution. Just as even the best physician encounters patients he cannot save, the best teachers will encounter situations for which there are no answers.

Once students realize that success in a program does not depend on the ability to reproduce course content on tests but, rather, on the ability to solve teaching problems, there will be a visible change in what and how they study. Presently most students study whatever they think they need to know in order to get a high grade--that is, what they think will be covered on the course examination. Since the skills and knowledge measured by the assessment exercises mentioned above so closely resemble those needed for successful practice of teaching, studying for an assessment exercise will be indistinguishable from studying to become a better teacher. Unlike many graduates of existing programs, who say that nothing they learned from the programs is relevant to success in teaching, students who graduate from an outcomes-based teacher preparation program will see the relevance of what they learn quite clearly.

Unless students in college-level teacher preparation programs do acquire knowledge relevant to successful teaching, knowledge which cannot be acquired better on the job, it is difficult to justify their existence. Both Smith and Clark (loc. cit) argue convincingly that such a body of knowledge exists and is growing. Its nature and importance were described eloquently in the report of the bicentennial commission of the American Association of Colleges for Teacher Education (Howsam, et. al., 1976). The real problem, then, is to convince the public that such knowledge exists and that our graduates possess it. This is precisely what the outcomes based teacher preparation program is designed to accomplish by documenting students' progress at every phase of the program.

RATIONALE

Many promising innovations in teacher preparation programs come and go without ever producing any visible increase in the quality of program graduates (at least not enough to convince me that there is something wrong with our basic approach to the program reform). I am convinced that the trouble is that we invariably concentrate our efforts on changing faculty behavior instead of on changing student behavior. Every teacher educator knows that what students learn from a teacher preparation program is directly affected by what they do while in the program and only indirectly affected by what their instructors do. Yet, every time we try to reform teacher education we seem to focus all our efforts on changing what we do, acting as if the necessary changes in what our students do and what they learn will follow automatically. The fact is that they do not. It is time to focus on changing what happens to our students, on what a teacher preparation program produces, intead of on the processes by which we try to produce them.

How do we change student behavior? The surest way is to change their ideas about what they must do to earn a high grade. When a student takes any course, the objective toward which he/she works most diligently is to earn a passing grade or better. Most students study hardest just before they are examined, and what they study is what they think will be covered on the test.

This is the principal reason why the assessment exercises I have described play so central in the outcomes-based teacher preparation program. That role is to direct students' efforts toward achieving outcomes which the program intended to produce. The principal function of the first assessment exercise a student experiences is to give a clear idea of what is expected of the student upon completion of the program, that is, being able to solve teaching problems.

A second purpose the assessment exercises serve is to make students aware of their own growth in the ability to solve teaching problems. Graduates of outcomes-based teacher preparation programs are not likely to say that what they were taught was irrelevant.

A third purpose of the assessment exercises is to change the instruction students get in the program by focusing it more directly and explicitly on problems teachers encounter on the job. As students begin to spend more time learning to cope with teaching problems, instructors will emphasize their instruction on these same goals and will become more concerned with relating research and theory to teaching practice. Faculty and students will find themselves working toward a common goal, and the role of the instructor will become more of a helping one. The real meaning of Oscar Wilde's asertion that "nothing really worth learning can be taught" will become clear.

A fourth purpose the exercises will serve is to provide visible evidence to the world that there is a body of professional knowledge concerning the practice of teaching. The fifth and final goal is to provide evidence that only teachers prepared in this program have mastered this knowledge.

IMPLEMENTATION

The success or failure of the outcomes-based program depends almost entirely on the validity, reliability, and practicality of the assessment exercises which lie at the very heart of the program. These exercises must yield valid measures of the outcomes the program is designed to achieve. Such measures should be reliable enough to support program decisions as well as decisions concerning individual students. At the same time, they must not be too cumbersome or costly to design and administer. This is a tall order but one that can be filled if we take full advantage of the state of the art of teacher assessment.

I do not claim that the solution I present is either the best or the only one possible. I only claim that it is one that can work. I also realize that after the build-up I have given to the problem, almost any solution I might suggest is likely to appear anticlimatic. So be it.

DEFINING PROGRAM OUTCOMES

One key element in the solution lies in defining program outcomes in such a way that they can be measured validly, reliably and economically. It would be presumptuous indeed to attempt to define these outcomes in substantive terms. What matters is the form of the definitions. Whatever these program outcomes are, they can and must be specified in terms of items of professional knowledge, professional skills and abilities, and professional attitudes and values which enhance a teacher's ability to cope with teaching problems.

Implicit is the assumption that teaching is one of the learned professions; that the role of a teacher in our culture is to apply professional knowledge, professional skills and abilities, and professional attitudes and values to the solution of educational problems. The outcomes of any professional teacher education program can be specified in terms of a set of **competencies** that each student is expected to acquire before graduating.

Figure 1 shows four basic types of professional problems a practicing teacher encounters; these are classified according to the settings in which they arise. Also shown are four types of competencies necessary for dealing with teaching problems. I suggest that any competency, any knowledge, skill, or value, included in a specification of program outcome would fit into one of the sixteen cells shown in the figure.

I have classified teacher competency into these particular cells to show that competency in different cells are best assessed in different ways, while competencies in the same cell are best assessed in similar ways.

	PREACTIVE	INTERACTIVE	POSTACTIVE	EXTRA-ACTIVE
PERFORMANCE SKILLS				
PROFESSIONAL KNOWLEDGE				
PROFESSIONAL VALUES				
PERCEPTUAL SKILLS				

FIGURE 1. THE DOMAIN OF TEACHER COMPETENCE.

Teaching Problems

Let us examine the four types of problems.

Preactive Teaching Problems. Preactive teaching problems arise when a teacher plans instruction; the setting may be at the teacher's desk, at home or the classroom; the essential characteristic is that no learners are present. Preactive teaching problems usually occur while learners are present but are solved in their absence. Deciding whether or not to use a particular film or videotape, and diagnosing a learner's reading difficulty are examples.

Interactive Teaching Problems. Interactive teaching problems arise while the teacher is teaching or interacting with learners in the classroom and must be dealt with under those conditions. Examples include: deciding how to answer a learner's question; whether to give another example; and what to do about a spitball that has just flown across the room are examples.

The terms "preactive" and "interactive" were first applied to these two types of teaching problems by Jackson (1965), who pointed out how different the competencies are which are necessary to solve these two kinds of problems are (Jackson 1965). I have coined two additional terms to identify two other types of problems encountered in the practice of teaching.

Postactive Teaching Problems. Postactive teaching problems occur in the same setting as preactive problems, but have to do with the teacher's own professional growth. A course designed to develop competencies of this kind, called "Reflective Teaching" has been described by Cruickshank (1981). Deciding whether one needs more practice in asking higher-order questions is a post-active teaching problem.

Extraactive Teaching Problems. Extraactive teaching problems happen when teachers perform professional duties such as meeting with parents or serving on the school's curriculum committee. These problems do not directly involve the teacher's performance.

Teacher Competencies and Teacher Performance

The role each of the four kinds of competencies plays in teacher performance, that is, in the solution of professional problems, is shown schematically in Figure 2.

Perceptual Skills. Kounin (1970) reported and emphasized the importance of perceptual skills in interactive teaching. He added the term **withitness** to the professional vocabulary of teachers. More recent work by Berliner (1986) has added to our understanding of this, the most basic kind of competency. No teacher can solve a problem when he/she is not aware of its existence. Developing perceptual skills is an important but often neglected part of a teacher's professional training. As the diagram indicates, failure to apply certain **perceptual skills** in the classroom makes it impossible to use any of the other types of competencies.

Professional Values. If a teacher is aware of problem behavior, she must also recognize it as such. I have used the term **professional values** to refer to this competency. A teacher who is aware of problem behavior but does not recognize it as such cannot solve the problem. Research reported by Berliner (loc. cit.) has confirmed that competencies of this type characterize expert teachers.

Professional Judgment. In addition to being aware of what students are doing in any given situation, the teacher should have a clear concept of what they ought to be doing in that situation. The competent teacher recognizes

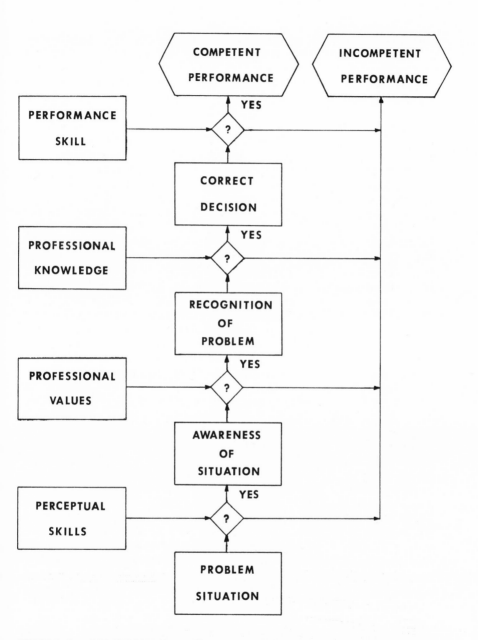

FIGURE 2. RELATIONSHIP BETWEEN TEACHER COMPETENCE AND
TEACHER PERFORMANCE.

when the two differ enough to create a problem.
I use the term **professional judgment** to refer
to the ability to do this. Research reported
by Berliner (1986) indicates that competencies
of this type characterize expert teachers.

Performance Skills. Finally, competent
practice of the teaching profession demands the
ability to apply professional knowledge, to
implement solutions to teaching problems.
     The rest of this discussion will,
therefore, be devoted to the problem of
obtaining measurements of teacher competence
accurate enough to substantiate the evaluation.
Becuse they are considered the most difficult
to measure, this discussion will focus
primarily on interactive teaching problems.

THE ASSESSMENT EXERCISE

The assessment exercise consists of a series of
teaching problems which students in the program
are expected to solve. Each problem consists
of two parts: (1) a **situation** in which a
teaching problem might arise, and (2) an **item**,
a suggested response or solution to such a
problem which the student is to evaluate.
Situations are recorded on videotape or film,
some in the form of brief episodes of classroom
behavior, others in the form of verbal
vignettes. Each situation is presented in both
audio and visual modes. The student's task is
to evaluate the items and record evaluations on
an answer sheet.
     It is, of course, impossible to create a
meaningful problem for the assessment exercise
without first defining the competency it is
supposed to measure. In practice, the primary
source of problems will be program faculty.
Each instructor will be expected to define the
kinds of problems students will learn to solve
in his course and what solutions will be
accepted. Courses will differ in the types of
problems they prepare students to solve, but
every course must prepare students to solve

teaching problems of some kind; otherwise, it has no place in an outcome-based professional teacher preparation program.

Examples:

Measuring a Perceptual Skill. One of the competencies to be acquired is the ability to recognize visible signs that a learner is puzzled or confused. Figure 3 illustrates a situation that might be used to measure this competency. This situation consists of a series of classroom behaviors recorded on 35mm film.

At the appropriate point during the assessment exercise, the filmed episode decribed in Figure 3 appears on the screen and runs long enough for a student to see what is happening. Then the picture fades and Item 83, the "response," appears on the screen. The student blackens the appropriate space after Item 83 on the answer sheet. Because the problem is an interactive one, the student is given just a few seconds to respond to the item before it vanishes and is replaced either by another item or by a new situation.

In this case, Item 84 appears next, and the student has a few seconds. Item 84 was designed to assess another perceptual skill. The parenthetical **R** at the end of Item 84 indicates that the segment of the film that showed the learners' faces reappears while the item is visible. This is done because of the possibility that a student who possesses the competency may have been paying attention to something else the first time the segment was shown. In the case of Item 83 no such help was provided. If most of the learners were indeed having difficulty, the student should have noticed it the first time the film was shown.

Measuring Professional Judgment. Item 85 is included to assess the teacher's ability to apply standards of conduct, a competency which falls in the area of professional judgment.

72

Film shows a teacher with a second grade
class discussing a bulletin board picture.

---

83. Most of the students were having difficulty
    with the main concept the teacher was
    trying to get across.

84. The picture was effective in getting the
    learners' interest (R).

85. The learning environment would have been
    better if the teacher had maintained
    tighter control.

86. The teacher asked at least one convergent
    question.

87. If the teacher had stopped to call for
    quiet, it would have taken even longer to
    get her main point across.

Figure 3. Measuring a Perceptual Skill.

Measuring Professional Knowledge. Item 86 is intended to assess some professional knowledge; specifically, knowledge of what a convergent question is. Smith has emphasized the importance of knowing something well enough to recognize it when it occurs in the classroom as well as when it appears as a question on an examination. (Smith, 1983).

Item 86 illustrates one of the risks associated with situations that involve film or videotape clips. Responding correctly to the item may involve more than one competency. It may involve the perceptual skill needed to hear the question as well as knowledge of what kind of question it is. If the student responds incorrectly, it is difficult to tell which competency she lacks.

The difficulty of determining which competency is being measured may be reduced in two ways. The method used in this example is to reduce the role of the perceptual skill by making the behavior easy to perceive; the episode contained not one but several convergent questions. Another way of reducing the risk of misdiagnosis is to include several items for each competency and base conclusions on all of the items, not just one.

Measuring Performance Skills. Item 87 is included in the exercise to assess a teacher's ability to decide when it is appropriate to use a particular performance skill--in this case, the skill of maintaining order in a classroom. Knowing when and when not to use a skill is important, but it is not the same as being able to command that skill when you need it. Only the first competency is assessable in this type of exercise. A major limitation of this kind of assessment is its inefficiency to measure the ability to use performance skills like this one.

It is doubtful whether some performance skills be developed during the didactic phase of a preservice teacher preparation program any more successfully than they can be measured

with the assessment exercises. The development
and assessment of such skills should be
postponed until the students begin their
internship, student teaching or whatever form
of practicum the program provides.

It makes sense to concentrate exclusively
during the didactic phase of preservice teacher
preparation on the development and assessment
of competencies of the first three types. This
is the most appropriate time to emphasize
research and theory and their relationships to
the day-to-day professional problems a teacher
encounters. Relationships between professional
knowledge, values and problems should also be
stressed. The ability to use such knowledge on
the job is best acquired later, after these
competencies are well established and while the
teacher is actually teaching.

Let us examine a sample set of problems
based on another film clip. This one shows
behavior in a high school science class. Item
88 is designed to measure professional
knowledge; specifically, knowledge of
questioning strategy. It serves to remind us
that this assessment exercise was not designed
to measure teacher effectiveness as such; it
was designed to measure how much students learn
in a program. This exemplifies knowledge only
graduates of this program are likely to
possess.

Item 89 assesses the student's idea of
what is acceptable student behavior while the
teacher is presenting, another professional
value. While the item is visible on the
screen, the segment of the film that shows the
whispering behavior is also visible. Once
again, this is intended to minimize the effect
of perceptual skill on the student's score.

Item 90 is another perceptual item, but no
part of the film reappears while the item is
shown. This reflects a decision to increase
the difficulty of this item.

Items 91 and 92 are both proposed as
measures of professional knowledge taught
somewhere in the program. The relevant portion
of the film is visible while the item is

```
---------------------------------------------
|                                           |
| Film  shows  junior  high  science  teacher |
| discussing a diagram of a fish drawn on the |
| chalkboard.                                |
---------------------------------------------
```

88. There was at least one teacher question which challenged the students to make a hypothesis.

89. As soon as the teacher noticed the two girls whispering he should have directed a question to one of them (R).

90. The girl at the end of the first row was more interested in the lesson than most of the other students.

91. The drawing on the board showed too much irrelevant detail (R).

92. The teacher's explanation of the way fish eggs are fertilized was procedural one.

Figure 4. Measuring Performance Skills.

displayed to minimize the effect of short term memory on student scores.

A Preactive Problem

This example illustrates a case in which the situation will not be presented in the form of a film or videotape of classroom behaviors. Problems set up in this form do have greater face validity than anything that is purely verbal, but the verbal format may still be best in some conditions. Information about the situation can be controlled better and sometimes communicated more clearly in this format. This mode of presentation adapts particularly well to the presentation of preactive teaching problems. Figure 5 shows an example.

Somewhere in the series of situations, one like that shown in Figure 5 may appear. Instead of a filmed or taped classroom episode the situation takes the form of a verbal vignette followed by a question about what the teacher might do. While all of this appears, a taped voice reads it aloud. When the voice finishes, the vignette and question stay on the screen while the voice reads the first of the suggested items, then pauses while the student decides whether the suggested action is appropriate or inappropriate and marks an answer. After a few seconds, the voice reads another suggestion. This is repeated until the student has responded to all of the suggestions. One, several, none, or all of the suggestions may be keyed as appropriate, depending on what students are taught in the program.

The format described above is particularly well adapted to assessing professional knowledge, because the problem can be identified so that the effect of the students' perceptual skills or professional values is eliminated. This problem was designed to assess the competency of knowing whether the child should be referred to the psychologist or not.

```
-----------------------------------------------
|                                               |
|  Gloria  does not seem to have any  friends,  |
|  although she is well-dressed,  polite,  and  |
|  pleasant looking.                            |
-----------------------------------------------
```

How might you help this child?

101. Take the first opportunity to speak to her personally and try to find out what her problem is.

102. Call on her regularly during class discussions.

103. Find out some special skill or talent she has and have her demonstrate it to the whole class.

104. Talk to her after school and suggest that she should be more outgoing and volunteer more often in class.

105. Get in touch with the school psychologist and arrange for him to see her.

Figure 5. A Preactive Problem.

The problem will be valid, of course, only if students in the program are taught to make such judgments.

CONSTRUCTING AN ASSESSMENT EXERCISE

The success of an outcomes-based teacher preparation program--like that of any other--depends almost entirely on the faculty of the program. It makes demands of them which are different from those made by an ordinary program. It requires faculty to specify the outcome of the program in much greater detail than any ordinary, process-based program does. And it requires each instructor to specify differently the objectives of his own course in terms of the precise kinds of teaching problems it prepares students to solve and to specify precisely what solutions will be accepted as correct. Each faculty member must also construct sample teaching problems for the common assessment exercises.

These extra demands will take time; more time, initially at least, than an instructor currently spends in constructing, administering and scoring whatever tests or other devices he uses as a basis for grading students. A workshop attended by program faculty and graduate assistants (if available) should be scheduled and devoted to the task. Following is a brief description of how such a workshop might be run.

After the necessary orientation, instructors and assistants responsible for each course should meet as a team to draft a set of problems, situations and responses, representing the outcomes of that course, that is, problems that can be incorporated into the assessment exercise.

Each work group would need to perform the following tasks:

o **Specify competencies** students should acquire in the course; perceptual skills, professional value positions, and professional knowledges. This may be done unit by unit. With one team listing as one competency the student's ability to recognize signs that a learner is confused, another might include knowledge of Bloom's taxonomy as professionl knowledge students should acquire in their course.

o **Define situations** that arise in the practice of teaching which provide opportunities to use each of these competencies; that is, that give rise to problems solvable by the use of each of these competencies. Some effort should be made to define situations of all four types, preactive, interactive, postactive, and extraactive. If a situation can be described in a brief vignette, the vignette should be drafted. If it needs to be presented by way of a videotape of classroom behavior, a description of what is needed should be written. The first example suggested above, calling for the ability to recognize learner confusion, would require a videotape. Problems requiring recognition of questions from different levels of the Bloom taxonomy, however, could probably be described in the form of vignettes.

o **Draft responses** for each situation of three types: (a) behaviors which a teacher might be expected to choose in each situation if she possessed the competency in question, (i.e., had learned what was taught in the course;) (b) behaviors which a teacher might be expected to avoid if she possessed the competency in question, (i.e., had learned what was taught in the course); and (c) behaviors a teacher might exhibit but which have nothing to do with the competence (such responses are included for the sake of realism). If one of the

situations was a videotape in which a
learner appeared confused, one type (a)
response might be: "give another example."
A type (b) response might be: "ask the
child who seems to be confused to go to
the board and work the next example."

o   **Key the responses** as correct if type (a)
or incorrect if type (b).

At some point all of the groups would meet
together and share the written vignettes and
responses developed. In addition to
suggestions for revising drafted vignettes,
members of each team should be able to write
additional responses to situations drafted by
other teams.
In this day and age the program staff in
most programs will have accumulated a
collection of videotapes of classroom
behaviors. At this point, the assembled groups
should view these tapes and look for naturally
occurring situations which resemble those
described by one or another team closely enough
to be useful. Once an excerpt has been chosen
for use in defining one situation, it is
usually possible to locate other useful
situations in the same excerpt.
Finally, a specification for the entire
assessment exercise should be put together.
The general format is shown in Figure 6.
This chart should show how many items in
the exercise have been constructed to assess
the competencies taught in each course. There
should be enough items relevant to each course
so that a scoring key can be applied to the
record of each student in the course to yield a
reliable score, which will replace the course
examination. At the same time, the range of
situations in the exercise should seem to the
student to be typical of those a teacher might
encounter any day.

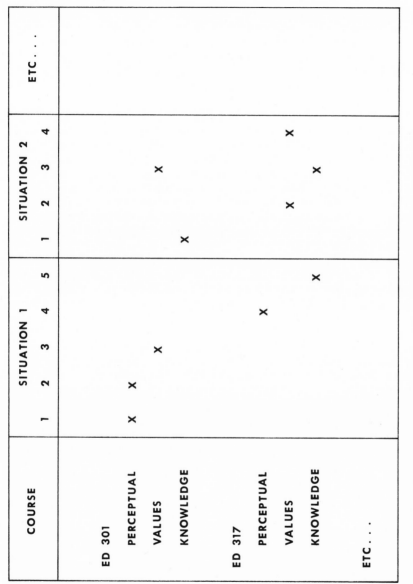

COURSE	SITUATION 1					SITUATION 2				ETC...
	1	2	3	4	5	1	2	3	4	
ED 301										
PERCEPTUAL	X	X								
VALUES			X							
KNOWLEDGE						X				
ED 317										
PERCEPTUAL				X			X			
VALUES								X		
KNOWLEDGE					X				X	
ETC...										

FIGURE 6. PARTIAL SPECIFICATIONS FOR AN ASSESSMENT EXERCISE.

82

Concluding Remarks

The student undergoing assessment is required
to make many decisions similar to those a
teacher makes, and to make them in rapid
succession and without as much information as
she would like, much as a teacher must. The
experience such an assessment can provide
someone who has never taught school and will
convince the skeptical undergraduate that
he/she has much to learn in the school of
education before becoming competent to teach.
It will give any entering student a clear idea
of what is to be learned in the program and of
what kinds of problems he/she is expected to be
able to solve before being recommended for
certification as competent to teach.
Additionally, if you can lure any local critic
of teacher education--a newspaper reporter,
perhaps, or a liberal arts professor--to sit in
on one of these exercises it may allay much
skepticism by giving them an amount of insight
that very few critics have.

Developing assessment exercises will
require faculty time, a more thorough
searching, a more explicit definition teacher
competence. They must also describe how
students can acquire such competence. This may
demand considerable more planning than most
faculties of education have traditionally done.
If I understand what B. O. Smith, Dave Clark
and other wise people are saying, the need for
such self-scrutiny has never been more urgent
than it is today.

REFERENCES

Berliner, D. (1986). In pursuit of the expert
    pedagogue. **Educational Researcher.** 15(7),
    5-13.
Clark, D. L. (1986). Transforming the
    structure for the professional preparation
    of teachers. In J. D. Rahts & L. G. Katz
    (Eds.). **Advances in teacher education:
    Vol. 2.** Norwood, NJ: Ablex, pp 1-19.

Cruickshank, D. R. (1981). Reflective teaching as a strategy for teacher growth. **Educational Leadership.** 38: 553-54.

Howsam, R. B., Corrigan, D. C., Denemark, G. W., & Nash, R. J. (1976). **Educating a profession.** Washington: American Association of Colleges for Teacher Education.

Jackson, P. W. (1966). **The way teaching is.** Washington: Association for Supervision and Curriculum Development and the Center for the Study of Instruction of the National Education Association.

Kounin, J. S. (1978). **Discipline and group management in classrooms.** New York: Holt, Rinehart and Winston.

Medley, D. M. (1982). **Teacher competency Testing and the teacher educator.** Charlottesville, Virginia: Bureau of Educational Research, School of Education, University of Virginia and the Association of Teacher Educators.

Medley, D. M., Coker, H. & Soar, R. S. (1984). **Measurement-based evaluation of teacher performance: an empirical approach.** New York: Longman.

Smith, B. O. (1983). Teacher education in transition. pp. 140-145 in **Essential Knowledge for beginning educators.** D. C. Smith, editor. Washington, D. C.: American Association of Colleges for Teacher Education, ERIC Clearinghouse on Teacher Education.

Smith, B. O. (1980). Pedagogical education: How about reform? **Phi Delta Kappan.** 62: 87-91.

ABOUT THE AUTHOR

Donald M. Medley is Professor Emeritus of Educational Research, Curry Memorial School of Education at the University of Virginia. He was formerly at Educational Testing Service, the City University of New York and has been a high school mathematics and science teacher. He received the Ph.D. in Educational Psychology from the University of Minnesota. He has published in a variety of journals and has published chapters in several books, including the **Handbook of Research on Teaching.** He has served as a Consulting or Advisory Editor to such publications as **Journal of Teacher Education, Journal of Educational Psychology, American Educational Research Journal,** and the **Elementary School Journal.** Throughout his career he has pursued research in teacher education effectiveness.

5

TEACHER EDUCATION FOLLOW-UP EVALUATION:
HOW TO DO IT

Jerry B. Ayers
Tennessee Technological University

"Only when we know why a teacher is effective--
as well as how--can we decide how best to train
teachers" (Medley, 1977, p. 6). These words
are even more true today. A student spends
four or five years in an institution of higher
education preparing to become a teacher. Does
the institution really know how successful it
was in preparing the student for a particular
teaching position? If the institution
recognizes a problem with its teacher education
program, does it have the empirical evidence to
warrant changes? The answer, at best, to these
questions is maybe.
      Since program evaluation has been one of
the most difficult problems facing institutions
of higher education during the past two
decades, effective systems for evaluation are
essential if these programs are to meet the
needs of the 21st century. Every state,
regional, national, and international meeting
of educators devotes a portion of its program
to the issues of educational evaluation.
Accountability pressures from legislators,
higher education governing boards, the public,

and accreditation bodies have all contributed
to this new field.

In January 1970, the standards adopted by
the National Council for Accreditation of
Teacher Education, which became mandatory in
1971, focused the attention of institutions on
the problems of teacher education evaluation
(NCATE, 1970). In 1976, the standards were
revised, putting even more emphasis on the
evaluation of teacher education programs
(NCATE, 1982). After several years of work the
NCATE standards for accreditation of teacher
education programs (NCATE, 1986) were
overhauled. The redesigned standards were used
experimentally during 1987, and their use
became mandatory thereafter for institutions
seeking reaccreditation or initial
accreditation. Also, more states are requiring
that institutions meet the NCATE Standards as
a part of the process for the approval of
teacher education programs.

In order for an institution to be eligible
for NCATE accreditation it must meet eleven
Preconditions (NCATE, 1986, p. 8). Precondition
4 is directly related to follow-up evaluation
and states:

> The unit keeps abreast of
> emerging techniques and regularly
> monitors and evaluates, both
> internally and externally, its
> operation, scope, quality of its
> offerings, and effectiveness of its
> graduates.

As a part of the initial accreditation
process the institution must show, through
appropriate documentation that it has:

1. Developed policies for conducting on-
   going evaluation review;
2. Completed within the last five years an
   internal program review or reviews;
3. Completed in the last three years external
   program review(s), including follow-up
   studies of graduates and employers; and

4. Considered and/or made program
modifications based on evaluation results.

Thus the issues related to program
evaluation and in particular follow-up
evaluation are becoming important to SCDEs.
These formal standards also emphasize more than
before the need for conducting follow-up
evaluation.

Since the requirements have been in effect
for almost 20 years, many of the problems with
program evaluation should have been resolved or
even eliminated, and follow-up studies of the
graduates of teacher education programs should
have been implemented. Models, plans, and
systems for analyzing the programs should be
available. However, a definite need for these
features still exists.

Prior to 1960 little experimental research
work had been carried out in teacher education
either to determine the characteristics of good
teaching or to measure them. In the early
60s educators devoted significant time and
resources to study teaching and the processes
of teacher education. By the middle of the
decade researchers had made available a vast
amount of information on instruction and the
classroom. This information could be applied
to the problems of teacher education evaluation
(Peck & Tucker, 1971). Griffin, Barnes,
O'Neal, Defino, and Hukill (1984) pointed out
that the period from 1970 through 1984 was
productive in effectiveness research and gave
educators a body of literature bearing a
significant relationship to the real classroom.

However, few institutions are conducting
adequate programs of follow-up evaluation. In
a given year 30% of all institutions are denied
accreditation for one or more programs by
NCATE. The most sensitive standards and the
ones that appeared to give institutions the
most difficulty were those related to program
design and evaluation (D. E. Christensen
personal communication, August 16, 1984).
Adams and Craig (1981) conducted a survey of
undergraduate teacher education evaluation

practices among institutions that were members
of the American Association of Colleges for
Teacher Education. Results of their work
indicated that about 53% of the institutions
were surveying their first year graduates
systematically, and only 45% were surveying the
employers of the first year graduates. More
importantly was the finding that only 11.5% of
the institutions were conducting follow-up
evaluations that included direct observations
of the graduates during their first year of
teaching. Three years after graduation less
than 4% of the institutions were continuing
with direct observation in the classrooms of
the graduates.

Katz, Raths, Mohanty, Kurachi, and Irving
(1981) surveyed the value of follow-up studies
for improving teacher education programs. Katz
et al. identified 26 significant follow-up
studies of teacher education programs. An
intensive analysis of the studies indicated
that they could provide useful information for
improving teacher education programs. However,
the studies had numerous methodological flaws,
and the findings were poorly presented. As a
result Katz et al. (1981) concluded that there
was "much to learn about how to make follow-up
studies more useful."

Zimpher and Ashburn (1985) reviewed the
research on professional development of
teachers and on the basis for conducting
follow-up evaluation. They specified that
other researchers have advanced a number of
reasons why adequate research and research
models have not been developed for conducting
the follow-up evaluation, such as lack of
interest on the part of the institutions and
their respective faculties, the limits on the
understanding of various phenomena associated
with the process, lack of resources, inadequate
funding, and lack of practical methodology.
These inadequacies have caused researchers to
become discouraged.

Although the works cited above may be
considered outdated, follow-up evaluation has
not significantly changed in the past several

years. Many educators and researchers are still
talking about how to manage a reliable and
valid evaluation. The impetus is there to do
it, but several factors inhibit institutions
from taking the situation seriously and
launching full scale follow-up evaluations.

This paper has focused so far on the need
for follow-up evaluation and what has been
researched in this area. The remainder of this
paper will be divided into several sections
that will examine some of the problems and
constraints on conducting a follow-up
evaluation, conditions that must exist in order
to conduct an adequate follow-up evaluation,
suggested models and ideas for getting started,
and finally some things to do and not to do
when conducting a practical program of follow-
up evaluation.

RESOURCES FOR CONDUCTING FOLLOW-UP EVALUATION

A teacher education progam is analogous to an
industrial process in which a tangible service
or product is produced. In a teacher education
program, the institution or the faculty begins
with the raw material, a recent high school
graduate, and transforms that student into a
finished product, preparing that student to
assume the role of a teacher in a school.
Although different organizations, the
industrial process and teacher education
programs can be compared to illustrate the
similar problems both organizations share. To
compare a teacher education program to industry
affords a viable example, and the business
metaphor helps explain the need for expedient
change and effective programs.

The first questions that many people ask
when they begin to plan for conducting a
follow-up study are, "What will it cost and
what resources do we need?" No matter how many
times these questions have been asked, there
are no right or wrong answers. Typically
industry spends about 10% of the retail price
of a product on quality control. Therefore, if

the retail cost of a coat is $100, then the
producer will have spent about $10 assuring
that the coat met certain standards.   A figure
of 10% is the general average for industry and
varies depending on the product.   Of the $10
spent by industry in the above example, 5%
($0.50) will be spent on the prevention of
defects, 40% ($4.00) will be spent on
appraisal, 30% ($3.00) on internal failures of
the product, and 25% ($2.50) on external
failures.   Thus, on a $100 product at least
$4.00 has been spent on the appraisal process
and substantial other sums on evaluation and
prevention of failure.

Two of the major problems in the
development and implementation of adequate
evaluation models are follow-up and the need
for sufficient resources.   These problems have
occurred particularly at smaller institutions.
Conservatively, assuming that the costs of
educating a student to become a teacher through
four years of college is $20,000, at least
$2,000 should be available for quality control,
and $800 should be available for the appraisal
process.

At the present time, we do not have $800
per student for four years to conduct
appraisal, nor do we have the other $1,200
available to prevent internal and external
failure and to perform preventative
maintenance.   If we did have the resources
available, an institution with 1,000
undergraduate students in teacher education
could conservatively have available $500,000
for quality control of the preparation program,
including sufficient funds for conducting
follow-up evaluation.

To request the level of funding that the
above figures imply is probably an unrealistic
argument.   However, these figures illustrate
that quality controls, adequate funding, and
other resources are needed in order to
implement follow-up evaluations, producing a
quality product.

If the product is to be significantly
improved, adequate resources need to be

available for quality control in a teacher preparation program. Although no definitive figures are available for evaluation costs, there is every indication that resourses are inadequate to have substantial evaluation programs and to conduct necessary follow-up evaluation work.

Placing a cost on conducting a teacher education follow-up evaluation is impossible without examining a number of factors on an institution-by-institution basis. An institution must consider the size of the target population; any communication costs; the salaries of the professionals associated with the project; and, if traveling is involved, the geographical dispersion of the graduates.

Hearn (1981) listed seven important points to consider in reducing the direct costs associated with follow-up evaluation. These included:

1. Take advantage of field based faculty activities. Supervisors of student teachers and others involved with inservice activities provide opportunities for faculty to collect follow-up evaluation data. Direct observation data can be collected to coincide with other business that a faculty member may have in a given location or area.
2. Data useful in follow-up studies can be collected at the time of exit from the teacher education program. It is essential that certain data be collected in order to correlate with information gathered in the field as a part of the study.
3. In some cases it may be necessary to limit data collection activities to those graduates who are within a reasonable geographic location in relation to the institution. However, care must be taken in sampling and in studying the data. Validity and reliability of the data is directly dependent on accuracy in sampling and in achieving the proper sample size.

4. If a particular school or school district employs a large number of graduates of one institution, it may be possible to evaluate everyone and reduce costs.
5. In recent years, much attention has been given to developing and implementing comprehensive state teacher evaluation plans. If the data and information is in the correct form, it may be possible to utilize this information in follow-up studies.
6. A major expense category for some institutions may be in the area of data processing. Through coordination, several institutions could utilize the same basic plan and the same scheme for data analysis.
7. A multi-institutional consortium can be formed. Institutions of the same general size and same general mission could work together in a consortium effort. There is some danger in this practice, since this might jeopardize faculty ownership of an evaluation plan.

Additional information about cost factors will be provided in the section dealing with possible models and their implementation. Again, costs are associated with the amount of detail and the degree of reliability and validity that an institution believes it needs to conduct a meaningful follow-up evaluation and to meet the objectives of the evaluation program.

ELEMENTS ESSENTIAL TO THE DESIGN OF FOLLOW-UP EVALUATIONS

After years of conducting follow-up studies, research has found that certain elements and issues must be faced. These are of particular importance to a successful program of follow-up evaluation. At least ten characteristics are essential to any good teacher education evaluation program (Ayers, 1986).

1. **The faculty, administrators and governing body of an institution must be committed to conducting program evaluation.**

The faculty must have adequate input into the program and be committed to the idea of evaluation. The faculty needs a sense of ownership. If an evaluation system is developed in a vacuum without adequate input from the faculty, the results of the effort may be lost. Since administrators do not often see the value of follow-up evaluation for improving the programs of an institution, the administrators and governing bodies must become involved in the project in order to have an understanding and to provide the needed resources for conducting the work.

2. **Evaluation in higher education must be viewed as a part of the total program and not as an isolated project.**

In order for an evaluation project to be viewed other than as an isolated research study, it must be made a part of the total operation of the institution. Sufficient resources must be allocated to the evaluation efforts, and, too, they must be made a part of the total daily operation of the institution. If an evaluation project is carried out in isolation, the results will not be used for program development and improvement.

3. **Evaluation must reflect the goals and objectives of specific programs and overall program objectives of the institution.**

In order for an effective plan of evaluation to be conducted, it must be based on the specific objectives of the program and the overall objectives of the institution. Specific objectives of a program are an inherent element in a desirable evaluation system. If the plan for evaluation is not based on general and specific objectives for both the institution and the program, the

evaluation may become a useless exercise, and
the results of the evaluation will not be tied
to any specific effort(s) that may have been
made in the program.

4. **Evaluation must be continuous and
   longitudinal in nature.**

In order for the evaluation of a program
to be meaningful, it must be continuous and
should be longitudinal. Evaluation that is
continuous will allow for any measurement of
changes that may occur in a program as a result
of modifications and for determining where
problem areas develop. Many institutions, over
the years, have attempted a "one-shot" follow-
up evaluation and thus have lost the value of
finding out if the results of their evaluation
lead to an improvement in their program and
ultimately in the product produced (i.e., the
teacher).

5. **Evaluation must provide for and reflect a
   knowledge of the state-of-the-art in
   educational research and measurement as it
   relates to a particular program.**

The state-of-the-art of program evaluation
is rapidly changing. With the advent of
teacher effectiveness studies, the past 25
years have seen the rise of much fundamental
research that can be applied to the problems
associated with performing adequate follow-up
evaluation. There is a need, however, to
translate the theoretical studies into usable
strategies for gathering and utilizing follow-
up information.

6. **Evaluation must reflect thorough planning
   prior to implementation.**

The implementation of an evaluation system
within an institution can be a difficult task.
Planning prior to implementation is essential
if the objectives of the evaluation are to be
recognized. Planning and implementation are

the most important elements to be considered in a follow-up evaluation. A later section of this paper will explore the issues in depth that are related to planning.

7. **Evaluation must reflect the most efficient use of resources for data processing, storage, retrieval, and analyses.**

Prior to the start of any major evaluation project requiring the collection of large amounts of data, an institution must inventory its resources relative to those available for data processing, storage, and analyses. A decision must be made at the start of the project about the amount of data to be collected and stored and how it can be retrieved. Access to high speed computers is essential if a project involves the collection of large data sets. Data storage, retrieval, processing, and analysis will be discussed later in greater detail under the section dealing with implementation of a follow-up evaluation plan.

8. **An evaluation system must include a component for effective communication.**

An effective system must be developed for communication with anyone closely associated with the evaluation project and anyone who will use the end results. The faculty must have input into the project because they will eventually be using the data. In turn, there must be effective communication of the results to the faculty. The most efficient way for providing faculty input is to make certain at the outset, the faculty believes that it is their follow-up evaluation project. The results of the evaluation project must be disseminated and used.

9. **An evaluation project must provide for a workable system of evaluation data utilization in program decision making.**

The success of a follow-up evaluation
project can be measured by how the results are
used. If the results from the project are not
used meaningfully, the evaluation program will
fail, and resources will be wasted. An
institution must develop a built-in system for
the use of the results of the evaluation
efforts.

10. **An evaluation project must have a component
    to assess the effectiveness of the
    evaluation process.**

Industry constantly examines the standards
and procedures used in the evaluation of its
products. A project designed to evaluate a
program should have an established system to
assess its effectiveness for gathering data and
making meaningful decisions. Therefore, any
project used for follow-up evaluation should
have a system in place for self assessment,
taking the form of an external review by
consultants, an internal review by the project
staff or other technqiue. Such a subsystem for
the evaluation of a program should be developed
at the beginning of a project. Such procedures
can serve to validate the total process.
Any institution implementing a system for
teacher education program evaluation and in
particular follow-up evaluation should give
consideration to the characteristics of teacher
education program evaluation outlined above.
As a result the institution will have fewer
problems and will have a more efficient system
that will be useful for program development and
improvement.

**PLANNING FOR THE IMPLEMENTATION OF A FOLLOW-UP
EVALUATION STUDY**

Planning for the implementation of a follow-up
study is important if a successful and usable
program is to be undertaken. As a part of the
materials presented in this section direct
observation of the graduate in the classroom is

a key factor in the operation of a follow-up system. The importance of observation will be discussed in more detail later in this paper. At least seven points are essential to the planning of a follow-up study.

1. **There must be cooperation between the institution of higher education and outside agencies.**

In most types of program evaluation, and particularly in follow-up evaluation, outside agencies need to agree on the type of cooperation that is needed and expected. Prior to the initiation of a follow-up study it is essential to obtain the permission of and to consult with school administrators. All parties (i.e., graduates, school administrators and the faculty of the institution of higher education) must understand what information will be collected, how it will be analyzed, the purpose(s) for which it will be used, and who will have access to it. In many areas of the country, it may be necessary to consult with and have the permission of the local teacher negotiating group(s). In some places extensive follow-up evaluation has not been possible because the local bargaining group for the teachers did not make provision for such activities in their contracts with the local school district.

2. **Appropriate methods for subject selection for the follow-up study must be used.**

Various methods exist for the selection of subjects to actively participate in a program follow-up evaluation. Katz et al. (1981) found that a principal methodological flaw in follow-up studies was the selection of subjects. The basic premise of subject selection is that the process must be a defensible system and should be consistent across years. Further, it is important that the participants understand fully what will happen and how implementation is going to be done.

Various techniques have been developed to insure that the graduates will participate in the follow-up study. All aspects of the study must be explained in detail, and there must be constant communication with the subjects to keep them informed about the visits and what is expected of them.

3. Appropriate data sources must be used.

Follow-up evaluation can be undertaken utilizing a variety of approaches. However, data sources must be wide and varied and must be anchored to the objectives of the teacher education program completed by the graduates. In the past many institutions have relied almost solely on the use of mail questionnaires as a means to conduct follow-up evaluation. Questionnaires were generally developed and administered to the graduates, their employers, and possible peer teachers of the graduates. Frequently these instruments consisted of rating devices that did not discriminate between the good teachers and the less able (Coker, Medely, & Soar, 1980). Data collected in this manner may be inadequate and of questionable value when relating the findings to the achievement of established program objectives. It is important that more refined means be developed and implemented if useful data are to be collected (Evertson & Green, 1986). A later section of this paper describes in more detail the use of such devices as observation instruments and other techniques for relating follow-up data to the achievement of program objectives.

4. Both qualitative and quantitative data must be considered in a follow-up study.

Both qualitative and quantitative data have places in follow-up evaluation projects. Quantitative data can be easily analyzed and used with inferential statistical techniques. Many times legislators and lay boards are

impressed by numbers. On the other hand,
qualitative data can be more useful to
administrators and faculty in program
improvement and development. Recently the
field of qualitative methods in research on
teaching has come into its own right and should
not be overlooked in designing follow-up
studies (Erickson, 1986).

5. Data collection must be conducted for an extended period of time.

The impetus for follow-up evaluation
usually occurs about two years prior to the
scheduled visit by an accreditation team.
Follow-up evaluation generally ends about a
year after the accreditation team has left
campus. For follow-up evaluation to be really
effective there must be a long range plan
developed, implemented, and continued in place
for an indefinite period. If these essential
facets are not followed and taken into account,
much valuable data can be lost, and the
momentum for program improvement will be
diminished.

Numerous patterns can be developed for
collection of follow-up data. Obviously the
best time is during the first year after
graduation. If the graduate becomes involved
immediately in a follow-up study, the
individual will probably remain with the
project over a longer period of time. It is
important to have yearly contact with the
individuals in the study, even if no actual
follow-up data are collected. It is crucial to
maintain contact with the graduates because in
our mobile society subjects for the study can
quickly leave the area or simply move to a
neighboring state and never be heard from
again. Other key points occur during the third
year and the fifth year after graduation. Some
research indicates that individuals appear to
be doing their best work during their third
year in the classroom (Ayers, 1980). Generally
after the fifth year, the data that can be
collected through follow-up evaluation will be

of little use in program planning and revision
because the effects of the college program
have generally been superseded by other factors
and influences.

The key to success is consistency across
time and direct ties to the objectives of the
teacher education program. An effective
program of follow-up evaluation is dependent
upon the use of consistent instrumentation. It
is better to use the same instruments over
several years than to change every year.
Consistency in instrumentation allows for
comparison of data across time.

6. **Adequate training for the personnel
   collecting data is essential to a
   successful project.**

Training personnel to use data collection
instruments in the classrooms of the graduates
is crucial to the success of a project.
Usually follow-up projects have been conducted
that employed direct classroom observation,
utilizing graduate research assistants and in
some cases faculty. Both graduate assistants
and faculty must receive training in the use of
the instrumentation, and they must be given
adequate backup support and clerical assistance
in scheduling visits and other activities.

7. **Appropriate processing, storage, and
   retrieval systems must be developed.**

The storage, processing, and retrieval of
data must be considered at the beginning of a
project. A follow-up study that involves as
many as 50 subjects per year will collect large
amounts of data. A decision should be made at
the start of a project concerning the amount of
data that will be collected and stored and how
it can be retrieved. Access to a high speed
digital computer is essential if a large scale
project is attempted and if rigorous
statistical analysis will be used. Presently,
work is underway through the Center for Teacher
Education Evaluation at Tennessee Technological

University to perfect the collection, storage
and retrieval of follow-up data. Systems are
being developed to collect data in the
classroom through direct observation, and the
results are entered directly into a central
computer facility, reducing some of the
problems associated with the manual data
reduction.

This section has presented some
information and hints that will be useful in
planning and conducting a program of follow-up
evaluation. Planning is essential, or the
project can turn into a disaster with a
potential loss of valuable resources.

FOLLOW-UP MODELS

Follow-up models in teacher education programs
have always been important and useful. They
have consisted largely of mail questionnaires,
checklists, and rating devices. Sandefur
(1970), at the request of the American
Association of Colleges for Teacher Education,
developed a model for the evaluation of teacher
education graduates. The model was predicated
on following the graduates for up to five years
after they entered the teaching profession and
to relate the results to the objectives of the
teacher education program of the institution.
Sandefur's model has probably become one of the
more famous practical, "how to" models for
program evaluation. The major element of the
model is evaluation of a group of subjects in
the classroom during student teaching, followed
by continuing evaluation during each of their
first five years in the classroom.

In 1973, Tennessee Technological
University modified the basic model developed
by Sandefur and continued to utilize it
through 1985-86 (Ayers, 1986b, 1986c). In 1986,
with the establishment of the Center for
Teacher Education Evaluation, work began on the
development of other materials that can form
the basis for follow-up evaluation models. The
work of such individuals as Nelli and Nutter

(1985) is influencing the development of the follow-up evaluation models. A long list of suggested models and procedures could be listed at this point. However, the reader is referred to the work of Ayers (1986c) for additional details.

At the outset of the development of a follow-up model, the objectives of the teacher education program must be examined. Next instrumentation must be located or developed to determine how well the graduates have attained the objectives of the program. More specifically the program needs to determine how well the graduates are performing in the classroom. Medley, Coker, and Soar (1984) have advanced the minimum conditions for valid observation of teacher performance that include four distinct steps. Each of the steps must be performed with a high degree of objectivity and are as follows:

1. Setting, defining, or agreeing upon <u>tasks</u> to be performed;
2. Making a documentary, quantifiable <u>record</u> of the behavior of the teacher while the task is being performed;
3. Quantifying the record, that is, deriving a <u>score</u> or set of scores from it; and
4. Comparing the score with a predetermined <u>standard</u>.

In order to make a satisfactory evaluation of a teacher, the individual must be visited in the classroom and observed in the process of teaching. This is the only true way to obtain an accurate picture of what is happening in the classroom. Then this information should be compared to the goals of the teacher education program. The key to effective evaluation is either the development or selection of instruments that can be used to collect direct classroom observation data, and therefore, can be related to the level of achievement of the objectives of the program.

During the past 15 years the model employed at both Western Kentucky University

and at Tennessee Technological University used
such instruments as Flanders Interaction
Analysis, the Classroom Observation Record, and
the Tuckman Teacher Feedback Form. The
institutions were sometimes criticized, in
part, because of the particular instruments
used to collect observation data. However,
these instruments provided data that were
useful in evaluating the objectives of the
teacher education programs of the respective
institutions.

Certainly other instruments can be used to
collect classroom observation data. For
example, Beegle and Brandt (1973) and Simon and
Boyer (1974) have compiled anthologies of
observation instruments. Coker (1978), Coker
and Coker (1982), Medley, et al. (1981),
Medley, Coker, and Soar (1984) and Dickson and
Wiersma (1980) have been involved in the use of
low inference instruments in collecting
observation data. The work of Coker and Coker
(1982) on the development and use of the
Classroom Observation Keyed for Effectiveness
Research (COKER) instrument appears to be a
promising way for collecting useful classroom
observation data that can be easily compared to
teacher education program objectives. The
Kentucky Career Ladder Classroom Observation
Instrument is another example of a low
inference instrument that may be of value in
collecting useful classroom observation data
(Galluzzo, 1987).

Instruments other than those requiring
direct classroom observation can be used to
collect usable information for program
improvement. Deciding what information is
needed and most useful dictates the types of
methods used in a total program of follow-up
evaluation. For example, mail questionnaires
can serve to collect demographic information
and suggestions for improving teacher education
programs. However, questionnaires do have
limitations. Either phone interviews or the
personal interview provide another avenue to
gain insight into the level of preparation of
the graduates and ways a program can be

improved. If time and resources permit, interviews with these individuals can strengthen the effectiveness of a teacher and the nature of the teacher education program.

In some instances, data have been collected from the pupils of the graduates. A number of instruments have been developed that can be used in this type work. Again, the reader is referred to such works as Ayers (1983b), Sandefur (1970), and Cooper (1983).

The key to an effective follow-up evaluation system is the selection and implementation of a plan that will gather information useful in determining program effectiveness and will help develop areas for program development. A useful model may include demographic data gathered through mail questionnaires; personal information obtained through intereviews with the graduates and their supervisors; an evaluation by the students of the graduates; and most importantly, using a low inference observation instrument to observe the graduate in the classroom.

Adequate planning of a follow-up evaluation program is critical to the overall success and use of the information collected. Although it is beyond the scope of this paper, the reader is reminded that some of the elements of systems analysis drawn from business and industry can be quite useful in planning and using all types of evaluation. The works of such individuals as Banghart (1969), Cook (1966), and Nadler (1981) may be useful and interesting to those implementing an evaluation plan.

THE DON'TS OF TEACHER EDUCATION PROGRAM EVALUATION

In this paper an attempt has been made to focus on some of the practical aspects of teacher education follow-up studies. Nevertheless, some of the don'ts need to be addressed. Gubser (1981) pointed out what he considered to be a dozen don'ts in program evaluation. Some of these apply directly to follow-up studies, and it may be useful to include some essential ones at this point.

1. Don't fail to evaluate entrance variables to a teacher education program and relate them to the results of the follow-up evaluation and to the total program.
2. Don't expect the evaluation of professional teacher education programs to always result in rigorous statistical data that can be interpreted with little judgement.
3. Don't use just one instrument or procedure. Diversify and provide checks and balances on the validity of the study.
4. Don't try to get by inexpensively. As was pointed out earlier, teacher education follow-up studies require resources if they are to be meaningful.
5. Don't fall into the trap of assuming that the assessment of a group of graduates in a follow-up study is the equivalent to program evaluation. Follow-up is only one part of the total package related to program evaluation.
6. Don't use only mail questionnaires unless this is a last resort. The value of mail surveys is questionable.
7. Don't ignore follow-up evaluation and feedback even if it is negative.
8. Don't assume that just because evaluation data is available it will be used by the faculty of the teacher education program.
9. Don't treat follow-up evaluation as an afterthought. There must be adequate planning in order to conduct the type work needed to be of value in program development.
10. Don't forget to evaluate the follow-up evaluation program. Even though this paper has not discussed this issue, it must be kept in mind during the development and implementation phases. Periodically the system must be evaluated and changes made as needed.

These ten points stress the don'ts of
teacher education follow-up evaluation. These
were included as a reminder that teacher
education program follow-up evaluation is not
an easy task. However, with reasonable
resources any institution can develop and
implement a program that will be usable in the
development and refinement of its teacher
education programs.

SOME CONCLUDING REMARKS

This paper has focused on some practical
suggestions and ideas concerning how to conduct
a teacher education program follow-up
evaluation studies. The paper is by no means
complete, but it will serve as a launching
point for institutions to begin the development
of their own studies.

Many individuals over the years have asked
the author of this paper for a copy of "his
follow-up instrument" or for a copy of his
"model" for conducting follow-up evaluation
studies. There is no one instrument, nor is
there any one model, that will serve the needs
of every institution. At one point it was
believed that four or five models might be
suitable for program evaluation in most
institutions in the country. However, after
lengthy studies, every institution must develop
its own model or system for teacher education
program follow-up evaluation.

Follow-up evaluation studies are not an
end to a means in evaluating a teacher
education program. Follow-up studies are only
one part of a larger model or system that is
needed to adequately evaluate a teacher
education program. If the United States is to
remain a world leader, the educational system
must remain a top priority at all levels of
government. In order to have adequate schools,
there is a need for resources including
teachers that are adequately prepared to enter
the classroom. Evaluation and improvement of
teacher preparation programs are key elements

to the continuing success of the schools as we
enter the 21st Century.

REFERENCES

Adams, R. D., & Craig, J. R. (1981). A survey
of undergraduate teacher education
evaluation practices. In S. M. Hord & R.
D. Adams (Eds.), **Teacher Education Program
Evaluation, 1981: Theory and Practice.**
Austin: R & D Center for Teacher
Education, The University of Texas.

Ayers, J. B. (1980, April). **A longitudinal
study of teachers.** Presented at the
meeting of the American Educational
Research Association. Boston, MA.

Ayers, J. B. (1986a). **Design characteristics
for meaningful program evaluation.**
Cookeville, TN: Center for Teacher
Education Evaluation, Tennessee
Technological University. (ERIC Document
Reproduction Service No. ED 274 650)

Ayers, J. B. (1986b). **Teacher education
program evaluation: A case study past and
future.** Cookeville, TN: Center for
Teacher Education Evaluation, Tennessee
Technological University. (ERIC Document
Reproduction Service No. ED 275 669)

Ayers, J. B. (1986c). **Study of the teacher
preparation programs of Tennessee
Technological University** (Report 86-2).
Cookeville, TN: Center for Teacher
Education Evaluation, Tennessee
Technological University. (ERIC Document
Reproduction Service No. ED 275 635)

Banghart, F. W. (1969). **Educational systems
analysis.** New York: Macmillan.

Beegle, C. W., & Brandt, R. M. (Eds.). (1973).
Observational methods in the classroom.
Washington: Association for Supervision
and Curriculum Development.

Cook, D. L. (1966). **Program evaluation and
review techniques: Applications in
education.** Washington: U. S. Government
Printing Office.

Coker, J. G. (1978). **A study of student teaching using direct observation.** Unpublished doctoral dissertation, Georgia State University, Atlanta.

Coker, H., & Coker, J. G. (1982). **Classroom observation keyed for effectiveness research-user's manual.** Atlanta: Georgia State University.

Coker, H., Medley, D. M., & Soar, R. S. (1980). How valid are expert opinions about effective teaching? **Phi Delta Kappan, 62**(2), 131-134.

Cooper, J. M. (1983). Basic elements in teacher education program evaluation: Implications for future research and development. In K. R. Howey & W. E. Gardner (Eds.), **The Education of Teachers.** New York: Longman.

Dickson, G. E., & Wiersma, W. (1980, May). **Research and evaluation in teacher education: A concern for competent, effective teachers.** Toledo, OH: College of Education, the University of Toledo.

Erickson, F. (1986). Qualitative methods in research on teaching. In M. C. Wittrock (Ed.), **Handbook of Research on Teaching.** New York: Macmillan.

Evertson, C. M., & Green, J. L. (1986). Observation as inquiry and method. In M. C. Wittrock (Ed.), **Handbook of Research on Teaching.** New York: Macmillan.

Galluzzo, G. R. (1987, October). **Evaluating teaching using a research- informed classroom observation instrument: A report of the Kentucky Career Ladder Pilot Project.** Presented at the meeting of the American Evaluation Association, Boston, MA.

Griffin, G. A., Barnes, S., O'Neal, S., Defino, M. E., & Hukill, H. (1984). **Changing teacher practice: Executive summary of an experimental study** (Report #9055). Austin: R & D Center for Teacher Education, The University of Texas.

Gubser, L. (1981). What not to do in evaluating teacher education programs. In S. M. Hord & R. D. Adams (Eds.), **Teacher Education Program Evaluation, 1981: Theory and Practice.** Austin: R & D Center for Teacher Education, The University of Texas.

Hearn, E. M. (1981). Finance and resource allocations relative to teacher education evaluation. In S. M. Hord & R. D. Adams (Eds.), **Teacher Education Program Evaluation, 1981: Theory and Practice.** Austin: R & D Center for Teacher Education, The University of Texas.

Katz, L. G., & Raths, J. D. (1985). A framework for research on teacher education programs. **Journal of Teacher Education, 36**(6), 9-15.

Katz, L., Raths, J., Mohanty, C., Kurachi, A, & Irving, J. (1981). Follow-up studies: Are they worth the trouble? **Journal of Teacher Education, 32**(2), 18-24.

Medley, D. M. (1977). **Teacher competence and teacher effectiveness.** Washington: American Association of Colleges for Teacher Education.

Medley, D. M., Coker, H., Coker, J. G., Lorentz, J. L., Soar, R. S., & Spaulding, R. L. (1981). Assessing teacher performance from observed competency indicators defined by classroom teachers. **Journal of Educational Research, 74,** 197-216.

Medley, D., Soar, R., & Coker, H. (1983). The minimum conditions for valid evaluation of teacher performance. **Journal of Classroom Interaction, 19**(1), 22-27.

Medley, D. M., Coker, H., & Soar, R. S. (1984). **Measurement-based evaluation of teacher performance.** New York: Longman.

Nadler, G. (1981). **The planning and design approach.** New York: John Wiley.

National Council for Accreditation of Teacher Education. (1970). **Standards for the accreditation of teacher education.** Washington: NCATE.

110

National Council for Accreditation of Teacher Education. (1982). **Standards for the accreditation of teacher education.** Washington: NCATE.

National Council for Accreditation of Teacher Education. (1986). **Standards, procedures and policies for the accreditation of professional teacher education units.** Washington: NCATE.

Nelli, E., & Nutter, N. (1985). **A model for evaluating teacher education programs.** Washington: American Association of Colleges for Teacher Education. (ERIC Document Reproduction Service No. 251 406)

Peck, R. F., & Tucker, J. A. (1971). **Research on teacher education.** Austin: R & D Center for Teacher Education, The University of Texas.

Sandefur, J. T. (1970). **An illustrated model for the evaluation of teacher education graduates.** Washington: American Association of Colleges for Teacher Education.

Simon, A., & Boyer, E. G. (1974). **Mirrors for behavior.** Wyncote, PA: Communication Materials Center.

Zimpher, N. L., & Ashburn, E. A. (1985). Studying the professional development of teachers: How conceptions of the world inform the research agenda. **Journal of Teacher Education,** 36(6), 16-26.

ABOUT THE AUTHOR

Jerry B. Ayers is Director of the Center for
Teacher Education Evaluation, Associate Dean,
and Professor of Education in the College of
Education at Tennessee Technological
University. Formerly he was associated with
the University of Georgia, Lenoir-Rhyne
College, and the Oak Ridge National Laboratory.
He holds the Ed.D. in science education from
the University of Georgia. He is the author of
over 100 published papers and has made 80
presentations at professional meetings. In
1973 he initiated the Tennessee Technological
University Teacher Evaluation Model. This work
led to the establishment of the Center for
Teacher Education Evaluation in 1986. His
current research interest is in the development
and implementation of models for the evaluation
of teacher education programs.

6

Pupil Achievement: The Weakest Link in the
Evaluation Chain

Doris L. Redfield
Western Kentucky University

The role of pupil achievement data in the
evaluation of any educational endeavor is
controversial. The public and publicly
supported politicians demand that the teaching
profession be held accountable for their
students' achievements or lack thereof. At the
same time, professional educators protest the
unfairness of accountability systems based on
student achievement.

The accountability controversy over pupil
achievement exists at every level of teacher,
school, and/or educational program evaluation:
primary, intermediate, secondary, and postsecondary. The current emphasis on student
test scores implies that, fair or not, pupil
achievement is the educational bottom line.
The illogically drawn conclusion seems to be
that teachers, not students, are responsible
for producing this bottom line achievement;
hence, teachers should be evaluated on the
degree to which they meet their responsibility.
If school teachers are to be held accountable
for their pupils' achievements, then it follows
that teacher training programs are to be held

accountable for the ability of their trainees (i.e., teachers) to effectively teach. Herein lies a very big problem.

The purpose of this paper is to address the broad question: How can pupil achievement data be used in the evaluation of teaching? In addressing this relatively broad question, parallels will be drawn between the evaluation of teaching in general and the more specific evalution of teacher education.

WHAT IS THE PROBLEM AND WHAT ARE THE ISSUES?

The Problem in General

Generally, an agreement has been reached among professional and public interest groups that the ultimate product of education is pupil achievement. However, little agreement exists as to what constitutes such achievement. Disagreements regarding the nature of achievement are certainly attributable to differential values within and between various interest groups.

The contexts in which the evaluation of teaching and teacher education programs occur are complex, multifaceted, and value laden. The goals and objectives of educational programs are determined by the needs and values of those served by such programs. Programs, then, are designed to result in specific goal attainment as defined by certain criteria. The criteria defining goal attainment, in this case pupil achievement, should certainly reflect the needs and values of those to be served by the program. Hence, program goals and evaluation criteria should probably differ among program participants within particular programs as well as among particular programs. Arguments about which evaluation criteria should be used and the weight that each should carry in an evaluation system implicitly reflect disagreements about the values influencing program goals (Gorry & Goodrich, 1978). Since

the values of program participants influence
both what is evaluated and the relative
importance of each factor evaluated, the valued
outcomes reflected in program goals should be
considered from the outset (Borich, 1980).

The public opinion voiced by policy
makers has generally accepted that pupil
achievement is best represented by standardized
achievement test scores. This acceptance
implies that academic achievement measured by
standardized achievement tests is the valued
goal and outcome of education.

Nonetheless, professional educators argue
the validity of using standardized achievement
test scores to evaluate their effectiveness as
educators. Their credible arguments include
the facts that: (a) standardized achievement
tests are designed to reliably assess students'
performance, not teachers' effectiveness; (b)
not all teachers teach subjects measured by
typical standardized achievement tests; (c) not
all teachers work with "mainstream" students
upon whom most standardized tests are normed;
(d) there are educational outcomes (e.g.,
motivation, self-esteem, prosocial behavior,
critical thinking) which are valued by teachers
and parents but which are not measurable via
traditional achievement tests and should vary
from class to class, (i.e., average performance
is not a defensible expectation for nonaverage
students e.g., handicapped, gifted,
disadvantaged).

The argument that student achievement test
scores do not validly reflect teaching
effectiveness is not meant to suggest that
teachers cannot evaluate their students'
accomplishments. As evidenced by various
teacher incentive programs or pilot studies
(Cornett, 1986), teachers can, and do, evaluate
their students, even outside the basic skill
areas. However, even when teachers validly
assess their students' achievements, that
achievement data may not validly represent the
teachers' effectiveness. Collecting one type
of information (i.e., student outcome data)
intended for one purpose (i.e., evaluation of

pupil achievement) and using that information for a second, unintended purpose (i.e., teacher evaluation) may seem logically appropriate; but, it may also be technically inadequate.

The problem, then, is not the inability of teachers to assess the quality of their students' accomplishments. Rather, the problem is determining the degree to which a student's achievements, however defined, are validly attributable to any particular source, such as, the teacher, program, socioeconomic status, or innate ability. This problem is often considered technical in nature. However, problem solution may be much more dependent upon adequately conceptualizing and understanding the problem than upon the perfection of some statistical technology. Clearly, there are many reasons why some students do not perform well; none of these reasons may relate to the teacher's performance.

Since we do not yet know how to directly measure teaching effectiveness, we are relegated to the use of proxy measures. While student achievement offers one proxy measure, it is not a particularly defensible one. Good teaching may be a necessary but insufficient ingredient in student achievement and/or student achievement may be a necessary but insufficient indicator of teaching effectiveness. Compared to indicators of student learning, observations of teaching behavior are more defensible as measures of teaching performance because: they are more directly attributable to particular teachers, and there is empirical evidence that certain teaching behaviors are positively related to student achievement (Anderson, 1972; Brophy, 1981; Doyle, 1985; Good & Beckerman, 1978; Kounin, 1970; Lockwood, 1978; Luiten, Ames, & Ackerson, 1980; Medley, 1977; Peterson, Marx, & Clark, 1978; Rosenshine, 1979).

Implications for the Evaluation of Teacher Education

The first question related to the evaluation of teacher education is: "What is the purpose of the evaluation?" Is the intent of evaluation to recruit and/or maintain students, if so, what kind of students--minimally competent or excellent? Is the program intended to train and/or maintain minimally competent teachers or excellent teachers?

Recruiting students and maintaining students in teacher education require separate efforts and evaluation data. Compared to the evaluation of excellence, the evaluation of minimum competence requires different cutoffs on similar measures, for example, factual knowledge in a curriculum area, and sometimes different cutoffs on other measures, such as, creative problem solving vs. basic factual knowledge. The evaluation goals of preservice teacher training would likely differ from the evaluation goals of student teaching, in-service training and professional development programs. For example, the emphasis in preservice training may be acquisition of knowledge. At the student teaching level, the emphasis may be on the application of knowledge. At the beginning teacher level, emphasis may be on the teaching and evaluation of subject matter. Among veteran teachers, emphasis may be on higher level thinking and personal development. Program evaluation must clearly reflect program goals.

No doubt the values of the evaluation participants will influence program goals. Hence, those values will also influence not only what is elevated, but the relative weight attached to each factor evaluation. Determining the purpose of evaluation suggests that differentially valued needs, rather than available methodology, are to drive the evaluation system. An advantage of needs driven evaluation is that it can serve multiple purposes. For example, if a need is that teacher education students learn the teacher effectiveness literature, then the degree to which that need is met can be assessed and the program modified accordingly. If a need is to meet accreditation standards, then appropriate data may be collected to show the degree to which the accreditation criteria have been met. The nature of the documenting data will reflect the values of those developing and/or implementing the evaluation system.

The importance of a needs driven system seems particularly critical when evaluating programs, such as teaching programs, which must function within particular social/political contexts (Craig & Adams, 1981). For example, differences among state statutes or philosophical differences between interest groups which support public versus private programs certainly influence evaluation needs. Those differential needs should, in turn, influence the development and implementation of evaluation processes.

A second question is, "Who or what is to be evaluated?" While the obvious answer may be, "the teacher education program" in many situations, program evaluation is, in effect, faculty evaluation. For example, a number of faculty may teach different sections of the same course so differently that the course is functionally different across instructors. In other instances, a particular course of instruction is "owned" by the only member of the faculty who teaches it.

A third question, then, becomes, "What constitutes the program?" For example, are general education courses part of the program? Are individual faculty and the courses they teach program components? Is student recruitment a program component?

Once the purpose of evaluation and the evaluation targets have been defined, the criteria for program effectiveness must be determined and operationalized. Just as it has been tempting to use pupil achievement data as the criterion for the effectiveness of school teachers and programs, it may be just as tempting to limit criteria for the effectiveness of teacher education programs which measure student performance. There is certainly a plethora of measures from which to select: grade point averages, standardized test scores (ACT, SAT, GRE, NTE), observations of practicum and student teaching performance, etc. In fact, different types of measures may provide differentially valid assessments at different points in the students' training.

If the task is to evaluate a program rather than individual faculty, then some legitimacy exists to using pupil achievement data. NTE scores given pre and post training could indicate minimum competence in the areas assessed. Behavioral observations of student teachers could provide measures of didactic skills not assessed directly by the NTE. If, however, the criteria for program effectiveness are limited only to measureable pupil achievements, then all measures of program effects are proximal; they may not be attributable to the program!

In a sense, program effects are analogous to school effect. Hence, the school effectiveness literature may suggest measures which, in conjunction with pupil achievement, may enhance the incremental validity of teacher education program evaluation (Good & Weinstein, 1986). Potentially useful indicators of school effectiveness include instructional leadership, high expectations for students and staff, strong instructional focus, and frequent monitoring of student progress (Brookover, Beady, Flood, Schweitzer, & Wisenbaker, 1979; Edmonds, 1983; Good & Brophy, 1986; Purkey & Smith, 1983). However, in considering indicators of effectiveness, it is important to realize that what may be an important effect for one program may not be important for another program.

To date, research does not support the hypothesis that there is one best prediction equation for pupil achievement, much less teaching effectiveness, across all teaching/ learning situations (Lara & Medley, 1987). Knowing how many relevant factors are operating

within a program may provide a more valid index
of program effect than knowing which factors
are present. Some stress theories and
substance abuse research literature illustrate
these factors. (Bry, 1983). The number of "at
risk" variables applying to a particular person
are more strongly related to dysfunctional
behavior than the type of at risk variables.
Instead of exclusively focusing on what we need
to have, such as, a particular set of
effectiveness indicators, it may be more
advantageous to consider what we have, such as
the number of diverse indicators in order to
demonstrate a program's effect.

What Have We Learned? What Are We Learning?

Schools, academic units, and colleges of
education have been evaluating themselves,
however loosely defined, for quite some time.
Despite this fact, and perhaps due to
editorial/publication practices, the published
literature on the evaluation of teacher
education programs is limited. Nevertheless,
surely a few lessons can be learned from the
evaluation literature in closely related
fields, such as teaching and school
effectiveness. Likewise, there is something to
be learned by recent state actions regarding
teacher and school incentive programs. Much of
the most current learning has not yet been
reported in the professional literature; it is
an on-going sort of learning, occurring in the
field-based trenches of various pilot programs.

What Have We Learned From the Literature?

When it comes to evaluating educational
programs, change or progress must be evaluated
and extraneous factors that may impact the
evaluated outcome must be accounted for
(Haertel, 1986). Recently, such recognition
has led to the almost exclusive use of
regression procedures for evaluating outcomes.

Pretest scores, or some other benchmark measure, are typically the basis for establishing expected progress on the criterion variable. Socioeconomic status and ability are two commonly used covariates. It is assumed that the variance in gains over time that are not attributable to the covariates may be attributed to program or teaching effects.

Multivariate statistical procedures have provided the technology for considering the amount of variance shared between and among numerous variables and achievement test scores. However, the seeming emphasis on the technology necessary for determining how to account for test scores may have distracted our focus from the real problem. Student test performance may, under certain circumstances, provide one indicator of student achievement. It may or may not provide an indicator of teaching effectiveness. It seems that our problem is defining the problem in the first place, not technological advancement.

What Have We Learned From State Actions?

Perhaps the greatest lesson learned is that effectiveness does not have a universal definition. Every state has, at least, considered establishing an incentive plan based on teacher and/or school effectiveness. When incentives are at the school or district level, standardized achievement test scores function as the major criterion variable. Regression models have been the most sophisticated means used to evaluate the achievement data.

When incentives are at the teacher level, standardized achievement test scores take a backseat if they take any seat at all (Cornett, 1986). Instead of test scores, teacher incentive programs seem to emphasize observations of teaching performance and evidence of professional development efforts, including the documentation of student achievement. Student achievement is broadly defined by these programs which include affective outcomes and may be evaluated in nonstandardized ways (via observations or self-reports which often have unknown psychometric properties). This is not to say that student achievement is being ignored as an indicator of teaching effectiveness. It is to say that achievement test scores are becoming recognized as necessary, but not sufficient, indicators of effective teaching. In fact, the city of St. Louis has shown that the courts will not support the use of student test scores to evaluate teachers. Lawyers for the plaintiff have not denied the need for teachers to be accountable; rather, they have argued that the use of students' test scores does not provide a valid indication of teacher performance.

What Are We Learning in the Trenches?

First, we (Student Achievement Mini Pilot, Kentucky Career Ladder Pilot Program) are learning that field-based educators differentiate between evaluation for awardiing incentives versus evaluation for facilitating professional development. In focus group interviews teachers have expressed the opinion that fairly objective evaluation plans can be developed and implemented and that those plans could contribute to their own professional development. The interviewed teachers would not mind being evaluated on the degree to which they had met educational goals negotiated between themselves and a knowledgeable instructional supervisor. However, they would not want personnel decisions--promotion, merit pay--to be based upon their attainment of those same goals.
    Second, we are learning that teachers having different levels of experience may have different expectations for their students and for themselves. It seems that mastery of content, mastery of didactics, focus on classroom management, teaching of basic skills, and focus on higher order thinking and affective outcomes may be differentially

emphasized by preservice teachers, student teachers, beginning teachers, and veteran teachers. For example, interview data gathered from veteran teachers indicate an emphasis on student outcomes which are broader in scope than the mastery of basic academic skills.

Third, professional educators do not seem to fear evaluation per se; rather, they fear unfair evaluation. Fair evaluation is perceived as dependent upon the evaluator-evaluatee relationship. It is important to teachers that the evaluator be a knowledgeable, professional, instructional leader with whom they can have a collegial relationship.

Fourth, there is a common perception that good teaching is probably recognizable by relatively naive observers; however, good teaching is probably not universally definable across grade levels and content areas. This perception reinforces the notion that not all effective programs may have the same effects (Berk, 1984).

Implications of What Has Been Learned/Is Being Learned For Teacher Education

The existing literature suggests that the evaluation of teacher education programs look for gains in criterion measures over time while accounting for variation in criterion measures that are not attributable to program effects. The covariates suggested by the literature (e.g., SES, ability, pretest score) will likely prove insufficient in postsecondary programs due to preselection processes. Two cautions are in order. First, different programs may desire different outcomes; hence, the appropriateness of criterion measures warrant careful consideration. Second, determining relevant covariates may be irrelevant. Accounting for variation in criterion variables may not answer the question at hand. The needs and values of evaluation participants need to determine the methodology, not vice versa.

State actions illustrate the importance of clearly identifying who or what is to be evaluated and the purposes for such evaluation. Clearly, the evaluation system must be defensible, unbiased, reliable, valid, and logistically workable. It is argued here, that validity may be program specific, especially if the evaluation system considers the needs and values of evaluation participants.

On-going work with field-based educators reinforces the notion that evaluation can, and probably should, have multiple purposes. Some evaluation has improvement as its goal and, as such, is formative. If a purpose of evaluating teacher education programs is to identify weaknesses for improvement, then formative evaluation is in order. However, using measures intended for formative evaluation to demonstrate accreditability or non-accreditability is not in order. For such purposes summative data are needed. Both purposes and data types should be considered in developing teacher education evaluation programs. Whether both purposes can be accomplished by the same system is debatable. Developing potentially effective, experimental programs may prove counter productive to summative evaluation by an accrediting agency. At the same time, such developmental efforts, if carefully evaluated and modified, may yield highly effective programs. Determining which program effects warrant summative decisions and which warrant formative evaluation should be driven by the needs and values of evaluation participants.

Field-based work supports differential evaluation purposes and, hence, criteria at different levels (e.g., pre-service training versus student teaching versus beginning level teaching versus veteran level teaching). In many teacher education programs, pre-service teachers focus on content-related and didactic knowledge. Presumably, that focus reflects program values. Those values, as emphasized by the program, should also be reflected in the program evaluation criteria. At the student

teaching level, a minimum knowledge level may
be assumed and the emphasis may shift to
application of knowledge. Again, this shift in
focus presumably reflects program goals and
should be reflected in program evaluation
criteria. At the beginning teacher level,
emphasis may be on efficient classroom
management and the teaching of basic skills.
At the veteran teacher level, efficient
classroom management and teaching of basic
skills may be given. Emphasis may then shift
to other domains such as higher cognitive
levels or affective domain. Such shifts in
focus, if they exist, should reflect goals of
teaching and should be reflected in evaluation
systems.

Fairness in evaluation seems to be a
critical issue when individuals are evaluated.
When programs are evaluated, fairness should
also be an issue. Even valid evaluation
criteria can only be validly applied when
programs are content valid and reliably
implemented. The integrity of program
development and implementation, then is a vital
component of the evaluation process.

Who evaluates what or whom is also an
important consideration in fair evaluation.
Teams who provide evaluators must be competent.
It may be necessary to include evaluator
training in the evaluation process.

Finally, good programs may be recognizable
by relatively inexperienced observers; but,
program goodness is probably not universally
definable. Goodness, like validity, is likely
purpose specific. There may well be a need to
identify those program elements that are
necessary, but not sufficient, for constituting
program goodness.

What Do We Still Need to Learn?

Various models exist or are being developed
(Haertel, 1986; Shulman, Resnick, Gifford,
Sykes, & Branscone, 1987) which may be tested
for applicability to the teacher education

evaluation dilemma. Testing existing, modified, or yet-to-be-developed evaluation models may require that we know: (a) necessary program effects regardless of program type; (b) effects that characterize the uniqueness of particular programs; (c) the extraneous variables that may impact evaluation results; (d) how to validly account for extraneous variance; and (e) how to interpret outcome measure variation that is not accounted for by so-called treatment effects despite experimental and/or statistical controls.

In order to determine the degree to which effect sizes can be attributable to any particular variable, we need to address the measurement by proxy issue. We may be able to show how much variation in student test scores is accounted for by any particular host of variables; but, those test scores are a proxy measure for the real variable of concern, viz., teacher or program effectiveness.

We may need to learn to abandon the mindset that affects sizes, based upon the partitioning of variance which can tell us the degree to which someone or something is effective. Perhaps the problem we face is not one of partitioning variance. Instead of trying to identify how much information accounts for the variance in a proxy measure, maybe we should try a holistic approach. Perhaps effect sizes are not as relevant as effect outcomes. We may not need to know the structure of a proxy measure as much as we need to know the functional outcomes of good teaching or good teacher education programs.

RECOMMENDATIONS FOR STOPGAP VERSUS LONG-RANGE SOLUTIONS

In considering problem solutions, perhaps we can gain from the experiences of programs intended to evaluate school teachers and school programs.

Stopgap attempts to evaluate schooling have relied upon the use of pupils'

standardized achievement test scores. Minimal
achievement of factual knowledge in traditional
content areas is certainly a necessary, overall
outcome of education but not necessarily
individual; nonetheless, it is not a sufficient
measure of the effects of schooling. Hence, we
have seen moves away from stopgap plans toward
the use of regression models to account for
effects other than schooling in achievement
test scores, pleas from professional educators
to consider measures other than, or in addition
to, standardized achievement test scores, and a
recognition by various states that evaluation
programs must provide for professional
development.

Implications for Teacher Education Evaluation

Stopgap attempts to evaluate teacher education
programs, like initial evaluation attempts in
the schools, have relied upon test scores. At
pre-service levels of teacher training, such
test scores may provide necessary, but not
sufficient, information regarding competence
for student teaching or certification as a
beginning teacher. Like our school-based
counterparts, we must recognize achievement
test scores for what they can and cannot
represent and interpret them in light of other
measures of program effects. Other measures
may include quality of lesson planning and
reliable observations of field-based classroom
management and presentation of content.

Long-range evaluation plans need to
carefully consider: the general and program-
specific intents of teacher education, the
criteria which best reflect program goals
across various levels of teacher development,
appropriate methods for evaluating and
interpreting program effects, and the intended
beneficiaries of the evaluation results. While
the first three considerations have been
addressed throughout this paper, the fourth
consideration warrants additional comment.

Some parallels can be made between faculty and program evaluation in higher education. It has been argued that faculty evaluation has multipurposes (e.g., personnel decisions versus professional development). Hence, there are multiple evaluation audiences, each of which needs different sorts of evaluation data (Peterson, Gunne, Miller, & Rivera, 1984). Program evaluation may also have multiple purposes (e.g., accreditation versus program development); hence, program evaluation audiences may be multiple and each audience may require different sorts of evaluation data.

In the evaluation of faculty, administrators need summative evaluation data and should probably receive only those quantitative data directly related to published standards for promotion and tenure (number of publications, number of committees served, number of hours taught, etc.). On the other hand, faculty may need information for improving instruction. Such information should contribute to professional development but should not be allowed to cloud the administrator's summative evaluation. Perhaps such information should be given only to faculty and their cohorts in professional development. Finally, students who are the consumers in the educational marketplace may best profit from descriptive information provided by their peers which would not be used for summative evaluation purposes and might or might not be used by faculty for personal development. In selecting classes students might profit from knowing a teachers' presentation style. Such information could be far more useful than knowing that a particular teacher is a 4 on a 5-point scale of teaching style.

In the evaluation of teacher education programs, it may be useful to think of the accrediting agency as the evaluating administrator who needs objective data for making an objective yea/nay decision. Those responsible for administerinig the program including the faculty may profit most from formative information for program modification. Students of teacher education are entitled to descriptive information regarding the programs into which they select.

SUMMARY/CONCLUSIONS

Clearly there is a need, and an interesting number of demands, to evaluate teacher education programs. Meeting the need will require a commitment to long-range, rather than stopgap, evaluation programs. Considerations warranted by effective long-range evaluation programs include: (a) the nature of the measurement by proxy issue, (b) the general and program-specific criteria for program effectiveness, (c) the necessary vs. sufficient evidence for program effectiveness, (d) the various stages in the development of competent vs. excellent teaching, and (e) the needs of various evaluation audiences. The needs of various evaluation audiences must necessarily drive the methodology used to address those needs. Partitioning of variance may not be the method of choice.

REFERENCES

Anderson, R. C. (1972). Learning concepts from definitions. **American Journal of Education Research,** 7, 385-390.

Berk, R. A. (1984, March). **The use of student achievement test scores as criteria for allocation of teacher merit pay.** Invited paper presented at the 1984 National Conference on Merit Pay for Teachers, Sarasota, FL.

Borich, G. D. (1980). A needs assessment model for conducting follow-up studies. **Journal of Teacher Education,** 31(3), 39-42.

Brookover, W. B., Beady, C., Flood, P., Schweitzer, J., & Wisenbaker, J. (1979). **School social systems and student achievement: Schools can make a difference.** New York: Praeger.

Brophy, J. (1981). Teacher praise: A functional analysis. **Review of Educational Research,** 51(1), 5-32.

Cornett, L. (1986). **1986 – Incentive programs for teachers and administrators: How are they doing?** Atlanta: Southern Regional Education Board.

Craig, J. R., & Adams, R. D. (1981). **Use oriented evaluation.** Paper presented at the meeting of the American Association of Colleges for Teacher Education, Detroit.

Doyle, W. (1985). Classroom organization and management. In M. Wittrock (ed.)., **Third handbook of research on teaching.** New York: Macmillan.

Edmonds, R. R. (1983). **Search for effective schools: The identification and analysis of city schools that are instructionally effective for poor children** (Final report). East Lansing, MI: Michigan State University.

Good, T. L., & Beckerman, T. (1978). Time on task: A naturalistic study in sixth grade classrooms. **Elementary School Journal,** 73, 193-201.

Good, T., & Brophy, J. (1986). School effects. In M. Wittrock (Ed.)., **Third handbook of research on teaching.** New York: Macmillan.

Good, T. L., & Weinstein, R. S. (1986). Schools make a difference. **American Psychologist,** 41(10), 1090-1097.

Gorry, G. A., & Goodrich, T. J. (1978). On the role of values in program evaluation. **Evaluation Quarterly,** 2(4), 561-572.

Haertel, E. (1986). The valid use of student performance measures for teacher evaluation. **Educational Evaluation and Policy Analysis,** 8(1), 45-60.

Kounin, J. (1970). **Discipline and group management in classrooms.** New York: Holt, Rinehart and Winston.

Lara, A. V., & Medley, D. M. (1987). Effective teacher behavior as a function of learner ability. **Professional School Psychology, 2**(1), 15-23.

Lockwood, A. L. (1978). The effects of values clarification and morals development curricula on school-age subjects: A critical review of recent research. **Review of Educational Research, 48,** 325-364.

Luiten, J. L., Ames, W., & Ackerson, G. (1980). A meta-analysis of the effects of advance organizers on learning and retention. **American Educational Research Journal, 17,** 211-218.

Medley, D. M. (1977). **Teacher competence and Teacher effectiveness: A review of process-product research.** Washington: American Association of Colleges for Teacher Education.

Peterson, K., Gunne, G. M., Miller, P., & Rivera, O. (1984). Multiple Audience Rating Form strategies for student evaluation of college teaching. **Research in Higher Education, 20**(3), 309-321.

Peterson, P. L., Marx, R. W., & Clark, C. M. (1978). Teacher planning, teacher behavior, and students achievement. **American Educational Research Journal, 15,** 417-432.

Purkey, S. C., & Smith, M. S. (1983). Effective schools: A review. **Elementary School Journal, 83**(4), 427-452.

Rosenshine, B. V. (1979). Content, time, and direct instruction. In P. Peterson and H. Walberg (Eds.). **Research on teaching: Concepts, findings, and implications.** Berkeley, CA: McCutchan.

Shulman, L., Resnick, L., Gifford, B., Sykes, G., & Brascone, L. (1987, April). **Research implications of Carnegie Report.** Symposium presented at the annual meetings of the American Educational Research Association, Washington.

ABOUT THE AUTHOR

Doris L. Redfield, Associate Professor of Psychology at Western Kentucky University, was on leave of absence during 1987-88 to work with the Office of Educational Research and Improvement, U. S. Department of Education. She has previously worked as a school psychologist and classroom teacher. She received the Ph.D. with emphasis in measurement, research design, and human learning and development from the University of Arizona in 1980. Redfield has authored over 50 papers. Her current research interest is in relating pupil growth to classroom teacher competency. As a faculty member she teaches such courses as Psychometric Theory and Test Construction, Tests and Measurements, Learning and Development, and Child Psychology.

7

Reflections on Conference Proceedings for the
Center for Teacher Education Evaluation

Nancy L. Zimpher
The Ohio State University

Reflections provided in this summary paper are
a result of observations made during the May
conference sponsored by the Tennessee
Technological University Center for Teacher
Education Evaluation. The conference, entitled
"Teacher Education Evaluation: Missing Links,"
served as a forum for presenting multiple
perspectives on issues and concerns related to
teacher education program evaluation.
Specifically, the conference focused on six
major aspects of teacher education program
evaluation. Those six aspects included the
following: outcome assessment, candidate
selection, pupil achievement, program
evaluation, evaluation of the educational unit,
and follow-up studies. The Center for Teacher
Education Evaluation along with the State of
Tennessee should be complimented for their
initiative. The State should be complimented
for its creation of Centers of Excellence and
the initiative taken to highlight program
evaluation as a focus of its support. Tennessee
Technological University should be complimented
in allowing its own decade of interest in

teacher education program evaluation to serve
as a lightning rod for the interests of others
which has led to program evaluation across the
country.
    When the Center for Teacher Education
Evaluation formulated its agenda two years ago,
clearly a major purpose was to further the work
of its members and the work of other
institutions in refining the nature of teacher
education follow-up studies as one form of
program evaluation. Beyond this the Center has
proposed the study of alternative models for
program evaluation and to the extent possible
to serve as a clearinghouse for program
evaluation interests across the country.
    This initiative is one that was begun by
teacher educators many years ago. Following
the inclusion in the standards of the National
Council for Accreditation of Teacher Education
of the evaluation standard, institutions have
had an increasingly focused interest on how to
create program evaluation systems in
particularized and comprehensive ways. One
specific example of a teacher education program
was first characterized in the work of J. T.
Sandefur (1970) in his creation of a model for
teacher education program follow-up studies.
As result of the explication of that model a
number of institutions began working on
refining this design. Tennessee Technological
University was one such institution. Since
that time it has taken considerable leadership
in explicating the nature of follow-up designs,
continuing studies, and comparative analysis
and in sharing the results from these studies.
Along with TTU and other institutions across
the country, a network was formed in the late
70s at the University of Texas Research and
Development Center for Teacher Education,
referred to at that time as the Teacher
Education Follow-up Network. For some time
this organization served the needs of program
evaluators across the country who were engaged
in follow-up evaluation as one form of program
evaluation. This group was convened regularly
at regional and national conferences, and

members of its network wrote papers and shared
materials and system designs. Across the
country communication was fostered through the
network. As those in teacher education program
evaluation are aware, this network no longer
exists. It is, then, with considerable
enthusiasm that the TTU Center for Teacher
Education Evaluation can serve in a networking
capacity for the group of interested teacher
educators who want to continue their
involvement not only in refining follow-up
evaluation systems but also in the general work
of teacher education program evaluation.

Thus the impetus for this conference is:
to update our knowledge and information about
program evaluation and follow-up studies; to
focus on the six areas of interest noted above
by inviting scholars in to present information
in these areas; and finally, to bring together
a diverse group of teacher educators including
professors, deans, directors of field
experience, departmental chairs, state agency
representatives, and classroom teachers to
serve in interactive and reactive capacities
during the course of the conference. Happily,
a number of these representative bodies came to
the conference in teams, assuring some
probability that as institutional
representatives deal collectively with the
problems of teacher education program
evaluation, their efforts will be strengthened
at their home institutions.

Specifically, these 100 people came to
this conference on teacher education program
evaluation with two questions in mind: (1) How
do the ideas presented in the six papers, and
organized around the themes noted above, fit
together? and (2) What of these ideas can be
transported to the local institutional setting
and used effectively in continuing teacher
education program design? My role with regard
to these two questions and the ideas presented
in the six conference papers will be to speak
in a synoptic way about what happened at this
conference. First, I would like to describe
what I believe occurred at this conference

developmentally; that is, in terms of the derivation of definition which define our work in teacher education program evaluation and with regard to the process of teacher education program evaluation. Secondly, I will focus on a set of insights derived from conference presentations which have been offered from a set of scholars long active in the field of teacher education and program evaluation. Third, as I have reflected on insights offered and questions and exchanges engaged in during the course of the conference, I will present a number of themes that were generated throughout the course of the discussion that can inform our work in program evaluation. And finally, in addition to obvious themes entered into the conference dialogue, I have a few observations about issues that were absent from our discussion which, as offered here, might provide some guidance for our continuing dialogue in teacher education program evaluation.

THE DEVELOPMENTAL ASPECTS OF THE CONFERENCE

I have chosen to look at this conference developmentally because as the papers were presented, as the small groups were formed, and as the dialogue began to unfold, I could see that we were assisting each other in our thinking not only by formal presentations but also by the interaction of speakers who had read each other's papers and by the reactions of conference participants. I saw the development of the conference on two fronts: first, definitionally and second, in terms of the entire teacher education program evaluation enterprise.

With regard to our development definitionally, Donald Medley prompted our thinking with regard to defining three terms. Early in the conference he differentiated among these three terms: competence (what a teacher is able to do as a result of graduating from a teacher education program); performance (what are the characteristics of teaching and the teaching context [that is, what are teachers able to do]); and third, effectiveness (what are the consequences of what teachers do with regard to pupil achievement and outcomes). Medley observed that he was interested in specifications of competence and that he was provoked to clarify what he was about after having read Schalock's paper. Schalock observed that teaching is fundamentally a matter of predicting success in job performance. As it later turned out in the conference, by Schalock's own observation, Don Medley had differentiated to three terms. Schalock is interested in an assessment of effectiveness as well, that is, the ability to relate the teacher's performance to pupil achievement and pupil outcomes. Schalock also extended the use of the term effectiveness to include conceptions of teacher productivity. Doris Redfield also found Medley's distinctions helpful since she was able to focus on pupil achievement and teacher candidate achievement as conceptions of effectiveness. Effectiveness was also differentiated by Raths as a distinction between educational goals as limitedly construed as student or pupil performance on achievement tests (either normed or criterion-referenced) as opposed to a focus on the growth and development of children and, to use Rath's words, "the betterment of the human condition."

My point here is that conference presenters and participants allowed us to see that clarification of language would help focus our efforts. Knowing whether and in what ways we are about documenting competence versus performance versus effectiveness will help us. It is assumed we should better clarify our goals and activities with regard to program evaluation.

A second developmental perspective which occurred in the conference was that the totality of the conference could be seen as emphasizing the interaction between different phases of the teacher education program evaluation endeavor. This developmental perspective is recorded in Figure 1 to show the ways in which various presenters focused in on the totality of our efforts with regard to teacher education program evaluation.

In Figure 1, I have drawn what could be referred to as a continuum; that is to say, presenters were interested in the long term construal of our efforts moving from the left of Figure 1, the time in which we select teacher candidate/professional teacher performance on some measure of pupil achievement. Intervening in this continuum is the impact of the teacher education program and the contextual condition of the school setting where teachers ultimately practice. Having this continuum in mind, it was Doris Redfield who linked for us two questions of evaluation that pulled the continuum together. Initially, she presented her agenda in the form of a question:

How can we use **pupil achievement data** in assessing **teaching effectiveness**?

Ultimately during the course of her paper and in our discussions she transformed her focus and ours to a subsequent:

How can we use **teacher candidate achievement data** in assessing **teacher education program** effectiveness?

She made for us the link between the process of looking at pupil achievement data as some measure of teaching effectiveness and as teacher educators, looking at teacher candidate achievement as some measure of teacher education program effectiveness.

Schalock took perhaps the broadest brushstroke in linking selection with pupil performance. As a consequence he receives the longest arrow in the diagram on Figure 1, wherein Schalock asks the compelling question about teacher education candidate selection and the predictive validity of such measures not

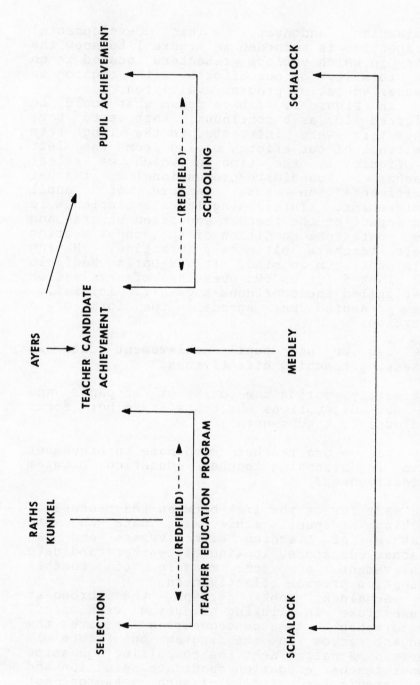

FIGURE 1. PORTRAYAL OF CONFERENCE PRESENTATIONS.

only in producing competent candidates as
graduates from teacher education programs, but
also more particularly teachers who can effect
increased pupil achievement as a performance
outcome.

Others as well at the conference placed
themselves along this continuum. Raths, for
instance, was exclusively interested in
formative teacher education program evaluation
rather than summative teacher education program
evaluation. Kunkel had a similar charge in
that he was looking at the school, college, or
department of education as the program unit of
analysis in teacher education program
accreditation. Medley, however, in contrast to
Raths, did take on the summative challenge and
looked particularly at outcomes assessment as a
form of teacher education program evaluation
concerning competencies of teacher candidates
and their achievement in teacher education
programs. Ayers used the summative perspective
as a point of departure to measure the
competencies of teacher candidate graduates in
the first several years of teaching. Here one
can see, then, in an attempt to bring some
animation to Figure 1 that there were
interacting and in some instance overlapping
areas of emphasis shown in the papers
presented. As a consequence, particularly in
regard to the central questions posed earlier
in this paper, the ideas presented interact to
constitute almost the totality of our
reflection on teacher education program
evaluation.

In summary, these developmental
perspectives on the conference provided
considerable insight to me, and I assume to
other conference participants. Definitionally,
I have a clearer perspective of how what we do
is differentiated, and how what we do needs to
be focused with regard to the intentions of our
program evaluation system. In terms of the
totality of the enterprise, it was helpful for
me to see that the six issues originally
generated to assist in the design of the
conference could be drawn in some kind of

portrait or synoptic view of the teacher education program evaluation endeavor.

DISTILLATION OF MAJOR UNDERSTANDING DERIVED FROM THE PRESENTATIONS

Let me begin this section of my reflections by applauding the Center for Teacher Education Evaluation in the selection of six outstanding scholars in teacher education. These people, though they work on different capacities or foci within teacher education, have much to contribute to our thinking about program evaluation whether our focus be on schools, or in schools, colleges, and departments of education; whether formative or summative; and finally whether we focus on competence, performance and/or effectiveness. Below, I offer a summary of these insights in an attempt to clarify what meaning these insights have had for me in my understanding of teacher education program evaluation.

Donald M. Medley: Outcomes Assessment

Medley provided participants initially with some remarks about the condition of teacher education practice in higher education and particularly public dissatisfaction with the ability of SCDEs (schools, colleges and departments of education) to produce bodies of relevant research as convincing evidence that a knowledge base for teacher preparation exists. In his caution and, therefore, call that teacher education programs become more outcome-based, he also provided definitions of teacher competence, performance and effectiveness and then spent the remainder of his paper on the notion of creating outcome-based teacher education programs with an emphasis toward the competence of teacher graduates in such programs. Essentially, he portrayed an experiential, problem-solving perspective on teacher preparation and in the description of this program provided a series of examples which illustrate the nature of competencies and the actual or simulated experiences which allow teacher education faculty members to measure the degree of competence exercised by these teacher candidates. Although there are many salient items put forward in Medley's description of outcome-based teacher education program design and assessment, one salient point rises above the others. He makes the point primarily that one of the most positive attributes of this program is that it specifies explicitly the competencies expected for teacher candidates to attain. The impact of such specification, as Medley notes, is as follows:

> Once students realize that success in a program does not depend on the ability to reproduce course content tests but, rather, on the ability to solve teaching problems, there will be a visible change in what and how they study. Presently, students study whatever they think they need to know in order to get a high grade--that is, what they think will be on the course examination. Since the skills and knowledge measured by the assessment exercises . . . so closely resemble those needed for successful practice of teaching, studying for an assessment exercise will be indistinguishable from studying to become a better teacher (pp. 4-5).

I gleaned from this observation that if the teacher wants students to know they have had a treatment, the teacher must tell them so. Not only will students be able to test a particular ability and demonstrate competence in the process, but they will also be able to express or articulate that they know they know. Not only does making objectives or outcomes for the program explicit, but also expecting students to exercise and practice these abilities, heightens the possibility of effective teacher behaviors. It also signals to a discerning teacher candidate, what the intentions of the program are, and therefore, what the intended behaviors of effective teaching are.

H. Del Schalock: Candidate Selection

The combination of Schalock's paper and presentation presented a powerful specification for the nature of teacher effectiveness particularly with regard to the performing abilities of teacher candidates. Schalock's charge was to look at the selection of prospective teachers and the predictability of their success in job performance. Relatedly, Schalock described the complexity of finding potential variables as measures of success in teaching and the predictive power of certain variables once isolated. As well, Schalock made a considerable number of points about the complexity of the school context and the dilemma of preparing teachers who might be able to exercise competence in a variety of settings. Schalock also dealt with the notion of the linkage between teacher performance and pupil growth as an outcome of effective teaching. In his presentation Schalock presented two major and rather unavoidable constants in the process of teacher preparation: (1) that there is a continuing and necessary link between teacher abilities and pupil growth, a principle we often stray from because of the difficulty in linking teacher education program effectiveness and student outcome measures; and (2) that teacher performance goes beyond a set of performances or competencies to a set of contextual considerations that make teaching skill necessary but not sufficient in the teaching/learning process. More specifically, Schalock applauded the notion of goal-based mastery learning and the role of teachers, not only in curriculum development but also in assessment. He cautioned against limited

measures of pupil growth, and he foreshadowed
the ever increasing necessity to link teacher
effectiveness with pupil growth, in spite of
the multiple contexts in which schooling
occurs.

Doris L. Redfield: Pupil Achievement

Redfield presented a paper dealing largely in
the methodological domain. That is to say, she
cautioned specifically about major questions
with regard to her central question which was,
"How can we use pupil achievement in assessing
teaching effectiveness?" In this treatment she
raised issues concerning the limitations of
certain paper and pencil measures of pupil
growth and development, the distance between
those assessment data, and the validity with
which one could represent the teacher's
effectiveness. She noted, "collecting one type
of information (i.e., student outcome data)
intended for one purpose (i.e., evaluation of
pupil achievement), and using that information
for a second, unintended purpose (i.e., teacher
evaluation) may seem logically appropriate;
but, it may also be technically inadequate" (p.
6). She argued instead that rather than using
indicators of student learning, observations of
teaching behavior are more defensible as
measures of teacher performance because they
are directly attributable to particular
teachers, provided that there is some empirical
evidence that these teaching behaviors are
positively related to student achievement.
Redfield also transposed her initial question
of the relationship between teacher
effectiveness and pupil achievement to the
restated question: "How can we use teacher
candidate achievement in assessing teacher
education program effectiveness?" Herein lies
the critical question for teacher education
program evaluation. She speaks rather
explicitly about the dilemma of linking pupil
achievement to teacher effectiveness and
cautions that it may be equally troublesome to

limit the criteria of effectiveness for teacher
education programs to measures of student
performance. She argues rather that we look at
program development in a more robust fashion.
Her caution ultimately is that we not reduce
our efforts in teacher education program
evaluation to effects that are essentially
proximal. That is using proxies for success
(pupil achievement scores or NTE scores) as
measures, of first on the one hand, of teacher
effectiveness, and on the second hand, to
outcomes that are not attributable to the
quality or lack therein of teacher education
programs.

James D. Raths: Program Evaluation

Jim Raths presented a teacher education program
evaluation process that focused largely on the
formative nature of teacher preparation
programs. As his charge was to look at the
nature of evaluation in schools, colleges and
departments of education, he set up a
hypothetical although somewhat common
conception of teaching as a helping profession
which guided the simulated experience created
in this paper. More particularly he used this
illustration as a way of probing the formative
teacher education program evaluation question
which is, "Are we doing it right?" and reminds
us that summative evaluation (which asks are we
right in doing it?) is not his focus. He
presented a model for faculty involvement in
planning for evaluation and analysis of data
(or paired comparisons) and strategies for data
collection which involved students as
informants and which encourage evaluative
activities as a main component of assignments
in an undergraduate course. Although Raths'
model was creative, I applaud his observations
primarily because he cautioned against one
major troublesome aspect of typical teacher
preparation. His concern was that programs
particularlize teaching and learning and reduce
it to the equivalencies of test performance or

isolate its skill orientation. This, Raths observed, is the difference between small verities (such as the teacher effectiveness skills of wait time, time on task, clarity) versus large verities (caring about kids, the betterment of the human condition, and a disposition toward teaching and learning). Clearly, he admonishes us not to oversimplify or to reduce the complexity of the teaching act to a set of technicalities which are embedded in the larger effort to increase and enhance the human condition.

Richard C. Kunkel: The Education Unit

Kunkel's charge was to speak specifically to the evaluation of teacher education programs from the perspective of the assessment of the teacher education unit (which one assumes to be schools, colleges and departments of education wherein teacher education programs are designed and delivered). Kunkel used as a point of departure a set of questions with regard to the definition of a professional unit, a blend of tenets for quality evaluation, the nature of accreditation as one form of evaluation, how teacher education accreditation focuses on the education unit, and some cautions and problems with regard to this analysis. Particularly his insights about program unit assessment, accreditation or evaluation were with regard to an analysis of the educational unit itself and his interest in meta-evaluation of the unit (i.e., the unit evaluating its own evaluation system). Here is the provocative point: not only does the unit evaluation focus on the program delivery structure, but it also ultimately focuses on the assessment of program evaluation during the course of accreditation proceedings.

Jerry B. Ayers: Follow-up Studies

The productivity of Tennessee Technological
University, with regard to its work in follow-
up studies as one form of teacher program
evaluation, has been well established. In
Ayers' paper, a historical perspective was
given on the evolution of follow-up studies as
one mode of program evaluation encouraged by
the National Council for Accreditation of
Teacher Education since the early 70s. In his
paper, Ayers gave definitions of the process,
described the necessary resources for designing
and implementing follow-up evaluations, and
enlightened the reader once again as to those
essential elements for conducting effective
follow-up evaluations. His treatment was also
enhanced by a number of cautions that are
likely to interfere with the effective conduct
of follow-up models. The enduring perspective
that should be placed on Ayers' work is that he
has taken one strand of teacher education
program evaluation and attempted to draw from
it in as many directions as possible including
an expansion of instrumentation, the execution
of both quantitative and qualitative measures,
the actual onsight visitation and observation
of teacher candidates in the early years of
their teaching experience, the reliance on
school professionals to assist in this
assessment and most assuredly the tenacity with
which institutions must pursue teacher
education program evaluation. I applaud Ayers
for taking a model essentially created over a
decade ago and showing over time the
complexities of trying to implement one good
idea. The documentation and chronicling of
these efforts at Tennessee Tech has certainly
been a demonstration of the commitment and
industry necessary to conduct teacher education
program evaluation.
    Observations drawn from these six papers
were first to offer general insight into the
nature of the papers, but secondly to tease
from the papers and presentations those points
of wisdom that could be enduring in our

continuing dialogue about teacher education program evaluation. I move now to a brief presentation of a host of issues that were recurring and made explicit not only by the papers and presentations, but also throughout the dialogue of small group interaction and questions and answers among and between the speakers present for the conference.

AN ANALYSIS OF CONFERENCE THEMES

There is no orderly way to present the most salient themes proposed during our day and one-half together. They are ordered largely in the manner in which they have occurred to me and are numbered, not to prioritize them, but merely to keep the issues separate. Further, I thank conference participants for raising the issues which I merely recorded as worthy of continuing reflection.

1. There was much discussion in the course of the conference with regard to the question of minimum competence versus excellence. There was concern that the design of teacher education programs, evaluation and ultimately measuring teacher effectiveness against whatever construal of pupil achievement would serve only the least or lowest common denominator. Relatedly in the face of great public scrutiny we are tempted to look for closure or summative data which give sense of precision about the way in which we collect data to measure teacher effectiveness while we squelch creativity, risk-taking, and variability across teacher preparation programs and teacher practice. There was even some concern that state and national mandates have been responsive to public fears and complex measures of teacher effectiveness. We are, as a number of participants observed, a profession where we need thresholds at a safety level. But we are cautioned not to stop at these minimal competencies but rather, to go beyond more simplistic and technical measures to more

complex measures. This was admittedly an unresolved but enduring issue in our dialogue.

2. There were repeated references to the notion of rigor in teacher education programs. In Medley's presentation a sense of rigor was evident in his description of the teacher candidates' need to know what we wanted them to know. Specification would not only bring competence but would also bring about some confidence that teacher candidates knew what they were expected to learn, and therefore, knew what they knew. Raths observed that learning takes effort and that teacher candidates as well as teacher education faculty could be encouraged to engage in a labor-intensive experience. Further, Raths was encouraging us to set standards in teacher education programs which would discourage the less heartened teacher candidate and reflect for all students engaged in the program a degree of difficulty in the program. He also emphasized rigor in the nature of teacher candidate selectivity, and there was a sense among conference participants that we ask a great deal of ourselves concerning the labor-intensive nature of teacher education, but we fail to expect the same investment of effort among our teacher candidates.

3. There was a recurring interest among conference participants and paper presenters in building shared conceptions of teaching which would inform the design of teacher education programs and ultimately teacher education program evaluation. This interest in shared conceptions of teaching did not manifest itself particularly in individualized or particularized notion of effective teaching but rather how faculty could collectively engage in discussions which would help them clarify the major purposes and goals of their programs. Medley recommended that faculty together identify the competencies in the outcome-based program he proposed. Raths used in his example a conception of teaching from Art Combs,

referring to teaching as a helping profession. Further, he proposed a process of "paired comparisons" which would be a way of generating some consensus about shared faculty goals and program design. Kunkel referred to some shared sense of mission in the educational unit which could be derived from shared conceptions of teaching. Schalock actually proposed a new perspective on teaching and schooling as a goal-based teacher directed educational system. Schalock equates this with a new paradigm of schooling for which schools, colleges, and departments of education should be preparing teacher candidates. In short, a number of the speakers proposed that the translation of some conception of teaching into a manageable set of knowledge, skills, and dispositions could move us away from specifications of competencies and a highly technicized view of teacher education curriculum.

4. There was some agreement among the presenters that the process of teacher education program evaluation is not the sole property in schools, colleges, and departments of education; rather, it is stretched or extended backward in the cycle to concerns over teacher selection as noted by Schalock, and forward into schooling and the engagement of teachers in the school context. This end of the continuum was discussed not only by Schalock but also by Redfield in her concerns over pupil achievement and by Ayers in his design of teacher education follow-up studies.

5. There was some attempt throughout several of the presentations to codify or capture the moving target of teaching or learning how to teach. Medley's construction of this codification was in terms of a matrix of 16 cells wherein he presented the domains of teacher competence, including the performance skills, professional knowledge, professional values and perceptual skills needed by effective teachers, and the contextual or situational opportunities for the explication

of these skills which are preactive (problem of
planning); interactive (the process of
interacting or teaching); postactive (teacher
professional growth); and extra-active (the
performance of special duties). There was also
some tension between the selection of promising
variables derived from the research on teacher
effectiveness constituted in the
process/product research paradigm as discussed
by Medley versus the confounding of the
teaching/learning process by the myriad of
contextual variables as differentiated by
Schalock.

6. I labeled this category the nature of
differentiations in thinking expansively about
teacher education program evaluation. There
was differentiation on at least three levels.
First paper presenters varied their focus on
the teacher education program evaluation
process by differentiation of the locus or
unit of analysis from pupils to teachers, to
teacher candidates, to program units, to
programs, to outcomes. A second
differentiation was in approaches to
evaluation, from particularistic processes of
evaluation, such as input/output models to more
holistic notions of teacher education program
evaluation, including not only process but also
contextual concerns. Another differentiation
was between the nature of formative and
summative evaluation and what are the limits of
responsibility with regard to these two forms
of evaluation vis-a-vis schools, colleges and
departments of education and elementary and
secondary schools. There was a fourth
differentiation in the dialogue, most
noticeably a paradigmatic differentiation
referred to on two counts: first by Schalock
who challenged us to consider a new paradigm of
schooling referred to earlier, and second to
two research paradigms represented by
quantitative scales and qualitative measures.
Kunkel went so far as to suggest that certain
phases of internal accreditation self-study
represent a quantitative review and other

phases, such as the site visit, represent more qualitative perspectives. Though this is probably too facile a differentiation of these two modes of inquiry, it does suggest that different groups have different evaluative functions. At least in these last two differentiations questions are raised about the epistemological orientation of teacher education program evaluation.

7. There was a noticeable tension among conference participants between some reductionists' view of teacher education evaluation versus a complexity of the phenomenon of teaching and learning and thus the measure of the effectiveness of teachers. The reductionist's view seems to represent an itemization of skills, a specification of prescribed observation inventories, with the acceptance of a host of rather explicit measures of teacher competence and pupil achievement versus a more contextual, person-oriented view of teaching and learning and a focus on human growth and development. Other ways in which this reductionist versus complex argument were reflected was in the productivity perspective on teaching versus the quality of our efforts. This tension recalls an analogical portrait of teachers as technicians or teachers as executive managers versus some other conceptions of teaching which include teachers as moral leaders, teachers as decision makers, teachers as scholars, and other images of these competing conceptions of teaching.

8. There was considerable discussion about the general issue of what constitutes program, that is a teacher education program. These notions ranged from what should be the unit of analysis for the teacher education program (the SCDE, the university, the university and the schools) to clear conceptions of teaching, the degree of rigor in the program, the expectations of the students, the organizational features, and the experiential dimensions of competence. One is left with the

sense that these and other variables ultimately may define the nature of program in teacher education units and in some ways this conference provided a beginning of some specifications of program design elements.

9. A final point is the reference, throughout the conference, to the collaborative nature of our work. This cooperation was fostered through references to the way in which a Center for Teacher Education Evaluation might work with cooperating institutions; to emergence of teacher leadership roles and the interests of unions in peer evaluation and the role of teachers in the evaluation of teacher candidates; to the evolution of induction programs as extensions of our teacher education preservice program efforts and foci for teacher education program evaluation; and finally to the evolution of institutional consortia represented by this center, institutions participating in the Holmes Group and national/ professional associations and other groups.

These items constitute some major and recurring themes that were presented during the course of the conference. I have attempted here not only to designate the item, but also in some way to explicate the intentionality of the item being discussed throughout the course of the conference. Now let me move briefly to a discussion of what might be called omissions or issues that were not but should have perhaps been raised at the conference, or might be included in future conferences sponsored by the Center for Teacher Education Evaluation.

ADDITIONAL CONCERNS

These additional concerns which are presented here simply accommodate our ideas and perspectives using alternative frames of reference to communicate with each other as we proceed in our very diverse but additive teacher education program evaluation efforts. My intention in this section is to simply propose frameworks which might be inclusive of the interests of the many people who are now engaged in teacher education program evaluation, teacher assessment, and school effects. The first is an encouragement to view the totality of our enterprise as "the professional development of teachers." This view suggests a continuum wherein we sustain an interest in a range of professional development checkpoints, or what is sometimes referred as benchmarks, from the recruitment and selection of teacher candidates, to preservice teacher education, to induction or entry-year programs and ultimately to the continuing inservice and professional development of veteran teachers (Howey et al., 1986). By viewing the totality of professional development against this continuum, we are able to see the range of ways in which we can talk about teacher education and ways in which our multiple efforts can be incorporated into a collaborative notion of what our professional development efforts are all about.

Secondly, it would help in our dialogue if we could differentiate teacher competence to keep in mind that teaching requires technical, clinical, personalistic, and critical competence. These concepts (originally presented by Howey and Zimpher, 1986) reflect necessary technical competence of teachers to include skills, knowledge, and dispositions with regard to highly specialized or individualized teacher competencies, such as active teaching techniques, engagement of student learners, item on task, wait time, and other promising variables drawn from the teacher effectiveness literature. Clinical knowledge suggests that teachers develop problem-solving and decision-making capacities and an ability to know about teaching diagnostically. Personalistic perspectives on teacher competence suggest that we have a knowledge of how pupils develop and how curriculum can respond to the personal motivations of student learners. It also suggests that we understand our own development as adults cognitively, morally, conceptually, and socially. Finally, teacher competence can be differentiated critically wherein the perspective on teaching fostered in teacher education programs and in schools is one of a teacher who is reflective, who is critical, who is a change agent, and whose epistemological perspective or way of making meaning out of the world is multiperspective.

A third framework that would enhance our thinking extends from the notion of obtaining an epistemological perspective to inform the way we come to ask questions about teacher education and program evaluation and the ways in which we select the measures which assess the efficacy of our work. This epistemological treatment was originally posed by Zimpher and Ashburn (1986) and suggests that the conceptions of the world and how we make meaning out of our experiences, in many ways suggests the direction of the conceptions of teaching most viable and most appropriate to our perspectives. If we look at a synoptic view of epistemology design, we are able as well to see models or alternatives to the positivisitic/empirical domain (from the process/product mode of inquiry) to more phenomenological, personalistic and naturalistic modes of inquiry and ultimately to some critical competence or ideological perspective of our work. This simply suggests that we might be able to incorporate multiple questions, certainly multiple perspectives, certainly the encouragement of students as informants, and the triangulated data collection needs in all of our teacher education program evaluation systems.

These frameworks are presented to extend our thinking, to allow bases on which we can incorporate new ideas and accommodate the ideas of others. It is synoptic in that it assumes that we might take the best aspects of multiple frameworks for thinking about teacher education and teacher education program evaluation in the conduct of our work. The conference has certainly been a clearinghouse for exposing the

problematic aspects of teacher education
program evaluation, and it has also been a very
enriching opportunity to think creatively,
collectively, to share ideas, to commit
ourselves to continued collaboratives, and
finally to answer the rather illusive
evaluative questions about teacher education
program evaluation.

REFERENCES

Howey, K., Matthew, W., & Zimpher, N. (1985).
    **Issues and problems in professional
    development.** Elmhurst, IL: North Central
    Regional Educational Laboratory.
Sandefur, J. T. (1970). **An illustrated model
    for the evaluation of teacher education
    graduates.** Washington, D. C.: American
    Association of Colleges for Teacher
    Education.
Zimpher, N., & Ashburn, E. (November/December
    1985). Studying the professional
    development of teachers: How conceptions
    of the world inform the research agenda.
    Journal of Teacher Education, 36(6), 16-
    26.
Zimpher, N., & Howey, K. (Winter, 1987).
    Adapting supervisory practice to different
    orientations of teaching competence.
    Journal of Curriculum and Supervision,
    2(2), 101-127.

ABOUT THE AUTHOR

Nancy L. Zimpher is an Associate Professor of
Education in the Department of Educational
Policy and Leadership, College of Education,
The Ohio State University. She completed the
Ph.D. at Ohio State and has been associated
with the institution for the past 15 years in
such roles as director of field experiences and
director of the undergraduate program in
teacher education. Her current research
interests emphasize the study of the
professional development of teachers and their
recruitment and selection into teacher
preparation through teacher preservice
induction and career development. As such she
has studied the nature of the leadership of
deans in schools, colleges, and departments of
education; the nature of program evaluation and
measurement; and the design and development of
teacher education programs. She has published
widely in these areas.

8

SOME MISSING LINKS

William J. Gephart
Tennessee Technological University

Donald Medley, the keynote speaker for the conference, worries along with us. He warns us of a powerful negative force at work both inside and outside America's public education system. Its goal is the demise of the system.

To become an education system "trasher" is fashionable. In "A Nation at Risk" we are told that rampant mediocrity is eroding the basic structure of our nation and culture. Since the beginning of the "reform movement" over 50 task forces, commissions, blue ribbon panels, and investigating teams have been created. Everybody who was anybody got into the act. And for every new study group a new set of voices declared that education, the public school system, was failing.

Concurrent with the reform movement was a perplexing decline of scores on college entrance examinations, measuring the "smarts" of each subsequent batch of cohorts inducted into the education system. When the scores dropped two years in a row, that fact was noted casually. When the decline spanned each year for five years, the pattern was noted with some concern. When the decline spanned eight years, reasons for the decline began to show in education literature. A number of explanations were proposed. More people are going to college, ergo . . . More blacks were going to college, ergo . . . The pill somehow was proposed as the culprit. The logic for this "cause" was so obtuse it doesn't merit repeating. Occasionally someone would say or write, "It's the test." And each time ETS responded convincingly. The test had the same psychometric features as it had a decade ago when the decline started. It can't be the test.

As the decline continued the annual Gallup Poll inquired about effects of the decline on the general public. The decline had a negative effect. As test scores went down so did faith of the general public in schools. (We know, of course, that the decline may be the cause of the public's reduced faith, OR it may be that the faith may be causing the decline, OR it may be that some other factor is causing both).

Another factor entered into the play. If people in responsible positions say something repeatedly, that something will be believed. If experts say often enough that our schools are failing us it will soon be accepted as truth: the public school system is failing our society. Year after year college entrance test scores declined and each year the general public's faith in the school system declined.

The test scores went down and down over a decade until there had been a two digit decline. Repeatedly explanations came and fell by the wayside. It isn't the test. It must be that our schools are not doing the job.

One potential explanation that did not get widespread consideration was a mismatch between the test and the curriculum it purportedly measured. The ETS was convincing. SAT had the same psychometric characteristics before, during, and after the decline; however, the curriculum had changed, and had changed markedly! Before the decline we had a rote curriculum. The big curricular studies of that time brought in process approaches to learning such programs as **Science: A Process Approach, PSSC** physics, **CHEMStudy, BSCS** biology, modern mathematics, and new approaches to writing. Adoption of these curricula gradually shifted the curriculum while the test stayed the same.

Each year a new group of learners entered the system with one more year of experience with a process approach to learning. Each year a new set of learners entered the system with one year more of mismatch between their curriculum (a process approach) and the test instrument designed to assess their aptitude with that curriculum.

As the test score decline gradually worked through the system, educators appeared to be particularly inept. We were party to a vexing problem. Our intellectual capability was deteriorating before our eyes. We had no believable explanation of what was happening: How long will it occur? Why is it occurring? And what should we do about it?

The test score decline bathed teachers and teacher educators with a residue of negativity. Nothing seemed to work! Our normally positive and creative colleagues seemed just as stumped as the rest of us.

Some of us rejected the degeneration that was washed over us. Some of us knew that the picture was not all bad. One by one those positive, creative educators among us began to step forward and announced a lot of good is happening in education. Phi Delta Kappa, the education honor society, set for its two year program an emphasis on the positive. Presentations by Ralph Tyler and other leaders chronicled two hundred years of successes in education. PDKs 600-plus local chapters undertook projects to uncover and promote the good in education.

Efforts help to accent the positive. Gradually we are winning back our professional status. Some of our critics assert that we lack a body of professional knowledge. That is just not true. There **is** a large quantity of professional education knowledge. (Non-believers should look at the **Handbook of Research on Teaching.** Each of the several editions has over 1,000 pages of references to research findings, printed in relatively small print). The body of education knowledge is incomplete. We don't know everything there is to know about teaching, learning, about a discipline to be learned. It is being added to rapidly by the conduct of educational research. And, because of a continuing adding of new knowledge, there is a need for interpreting the knowledge base and for re-interpreting the interpretation.

Just like medicine we have a body of knowledge. Just like medicine it guides us as we plan and carry out our work. Just like medicine that knowledge is large, incomplete, and expanding rapidly. Educators have a body of knowledge. It guides us as we plan and carry out our work, and it is continually being interpreted. We are in the same situation as the field of medicine. Both are inexact sciences in which standard practice is based on continuing interpretation of that knowledge base.

FORMATIVE AND SUMMATIVE EVALUATION

When we plan for the evaluation of education, **one** goal drives the planning. That goal is student growth in all its forms. These forms need to be stated. There are **two** general approaches for evaluation: formative and summative. Formative evaluation is conducted to assist in the decisions that will be made as a teacher structures and carries out teaching responsibilities. Summative evaluation is carried out to aid and inform administrators in making decisions about staffing, how they are going to assign, promote, improve, or dismiss me a teacher. Finally, there are **three** classes of variables that should be built into the evaluation planning: teaching style variables, (i.e., lecture, guided discovery, modeling, and simulation); employee variables, (i.e., punctuality, honesty, dedication, and ability to get along with other staff members); and student variables (i.e., intelligence, ability level, and socioeconomic status).

It should be thoroughly understood that **both** formative and summative evaluation need to be included in any comprehensive evaluation planning. And it should be known that friction often develops in evaluative work. As Michael. Scriven says, "Evaluation is nervous making." Recognition of that point gets us only half way home. Everyone involved in the planning and implementation of an evaluation has a responsibility to reduce threat in the evaluative work. We are all human beings and deserve humane treatment. No one has the right to treat anyone else with disrespect.

The most direct approach to evaluation of teacher education programs is found in the accrediting process. Unfortunately, that evaluation is in a state of crisis, needing to be changed. We need evaluation that is on-going, not just assessment at the end of a project or just after the NCATE visit. We need evaluation designed to help program planners and conductors make improvement decisions while the program is in process.

System analysis procedures should be the design guidelines for planning, implementing, and evaluating educational decisions. The work of Nadler (1981) should be consulted regularly. It should also be noted that systems analysis requires planning for change and for improvement in the future. Planning does not just happen.

Two more points need to be clear. They are evaluation in the "affective domain" and the role of "clinical judgement" in problem solving. There is much effect in evaluation. Persons involved in planning and conducting evaluation should be alert to those instances that produce effect. The system needs their assistance in putting those hidden agenda items on top of the table. Most of the time the candid, open presentations of situations will help reduce their negative component.

CLINICAL JUDGMENT

In some areas of endeavor, clinical judgements are readily accepted as a contributor to a decision. In education, we seldom fall back on clinical judgements. Our understanding of some phenomena is based on the systematic analysis of empirical studies. That understanding is enhanced when we carefully examine professional experience. We should not be in an either/or situation when it comes to learning. Knowledge comes from many situations. As a rule we should never discard any way of learning, for doing so puts restraints on what we know.

The complex of evaluation can be simplified and described in a 2x2x2 structure: (1) the two general approaches to evaluation, formative and summative evaluation; (2) the loci of the evaluator, internal and external evaluator; and (3) the nature of the data collected, quantitative and qualitative.

Formative evaluation is undertaken while a program is underway. Its purpose is to provide information that will help the program development staff answer such questions as what is working, what needs to be modified, and how can those improvements be effective? In contrast, summative evaluation is typically done when a project is completed. Summative evaluation focuses on questions about the degree a program does what it says it will. Summative evaluations want information on how well a program can be expected to work, with whom, and under what conditions.

The second factor that constrains evaluation has to do with the employment of an evaluator. Is it better to employ someone inside the system or someone external? The concerns here focus on the degree to which the evaluator can be free of bias. It is argued that the use of a member of the staff as the evaluator inserts bias. The individual works

for the same agency and knows all the people.
After all, the evaluator needs to be free from
those biasing factors. At the same time the
internal evaluator has an advantage in the
amount of knowledge concerning the entities
being evaluated. The internal evaluator is
there every day; whereas the external evaluator
is in town for a brief time in most cases.
Which should be used? That question should be
answered after a careful projection of the
impact of internal versus external factors.
Can we benefit most if the evaluator knows the
details of the project? Or do we need to have
a project in which we do not have to worry
about biasing factors?

A third constraining factor is the type(s)
of data wanted and used in the study. Here the
concern is for qualitative data versus
quantitative data. The major question of the
study helps resolve this choice. When
questions of generalization are pre-eminent,
the data with greatest objectivity should be
used. If completeness of depicting the
situation is the major concern, qualitative
data seem the choice to be made.

SOME CLOSING THOUGHTS

We have examined six factors that condition
teacher education programs and their
evaluation. Donald Medley began by recognizing
that powerful forces are ready to eliminate
teacher preparation programs. Medley clearly
states his position. He is a strong supporter
of the continuation of the multi-purpose
university and the colleges with them. That
support includes a recognition that some change
in those colleges of education is vital.
Central to that change was a call for
measurement-based teacher education and
measurement-based evaluation of teaching and
teacher education.

Medley proposed the addition of a
continuing problem seminar. Teachers need to
know about educational problems they will

encounter and about ways of resolving those problems. Teacher candidates learn about education theory, history, and psychology but not about problems and their solution, the every day activities in the schools.

Selecting teacher education candidates was the focus of Del Schalock. He characterized becoming a teacher as a series of predictions. At the close of his presentation he recognizes that our measuring tools are too weak to do the job success prediction. He calls on measurement specialists to help remedy that problem.

Doris Redfield focused on pupil achievement which she describes as the weakest of the missing links. The problem is that we are concerned with different learning targets. One group of learners is the elementary and secondary students. The other is the college students preparing to teach or teacher candidates preparing to nurture learning. At either level, the problem is defined in terms of pupil achievement as a proxy measure in assessment of teaching.

The program was the focus of James Raths. He outlined the many kinds of circumstances that teacher candidates should experience. One of his suggestions is similar to Medley's problem seminar. Raths discussed some measurement tools or techniques that teacher educators might use.

Richard Kunkel's target was the educational unit, the institution in which the teacher education program resides and functions. For evaluation purposes the education unit is the college, school, department or other administrative body within the institution that is officially responsible for the preparation of teachers and other professional education personnel.

Finally, follow-up explores the conduct of studies about education unit graduates. Follow-up is done for one of several purposes. The administrators of the education unit should know what those purposes are and for what purpose(s) follow-up studies are being done.

Jerry Ayers reported on 14 years of follow-up experience. His paper is the practical highlight of the session.

Accreditation by NCATE has been redesigned as of 1986. Prior to that, only one of the NCATE standards called for a follow-up study, which seemed to get lost along the way. Through the redesign, a major shift has been worked. Evaluation's role in accreditation has become clear throughout the accrediting process. Ayers' experience in this realm is clear. The bulk of his paper presents guidelines, techniques, tips and things to avoid. The reader will find Ayers' presentation a gold mine of practical suggestions.

The Center for Teacher Education Evaluation structured the conference in an effort to pull together the state-of-the-art in the evaluation of teacher education programs. The CTEE deeply appreciates the contributions of the 100 plus participants. And it hopes that future cooperative efforts may reduce some of the missing links.

REFERENCES

Nadler, G. (1981). **The planning and design process.** New York: John Wiley.

National Council for the Accreditation of Teacher Education. (1986, October). **Standards, Procedures, Policies for Accreditation of Professional Education Units.** Washington: NCATE.

Phi Delta Kappa. (1981). American public education: A 200 year perspective. **PDK Biennial Council Proceedings.** Bloomington, IN: Phi Delta Kappa.

Tyler, R. (1981). **Successor of public education: A 200 year perspective.** Bloomington, IN.: Ph Delta Kappa.

Wittrock, M. C. **Handbook of research on teaching.** New York: Macmillan.

ABOUT THE AUTHOR

William J. Gephart is a Senior Researcher with
the Center for Teacher Education Evaluation and
Professor of Counselor Education, College of
Education, Tennessee Technological University.
He previously directed the Center on
Evaluation, Development, and Research at Phi
Delta Kappa and has been a faculty member at
The Ohio State University, University of
Wisconsin-Milwaukee, and an adjunct professor
at Indiana University and Ohio State. He was a
high school teacher, counselor and
administrator. He received the Ph.D. from The
Ohio State University in 1965. He has authored
or edited over 200 articles, books, and meeting
presentations on research methodology and
evaluation. His current research interest is
in the development and implementation of models
for the evaluation and improvement of teacher
education programs.

Index